GOD'S WORD IN MY MOUTH

Colin Dye

Dovewell Publications

Dovewell Publications
PO Box 9161
London
W3 6GS
England

Scriptural quotations are from the New King James Version, Thomas Nelson Inc., 1991.

ISBN 1 898 444 80 3

Designed and produced by Gazelle Creative Productions Ltd,
Concorde House, Grenville Place, Mill Hill, London, NW7 3SA

My words
which I have put in your mouth
shall not depart from your mouth

Isaiah 59:21

CONTENTS

Part One

THE LIVING WORD

1

God's Word at work

God's Word is not a dated-and-dusty old book; it's the dynamic way that God communicates with you today. Without the living guidance of His Word, you can't move an inch in the direction of God.

With the Word's help, however, you can understand and fulfil all God's divine purposes. When the Word dominates your being, you can overcome *all* the daily challenges of modern life.

The Word is carried to you from God on His breath - on His Spirit. This means that it always comes with God's own creative power. The Word contains all the power that it needs for its own fulfilment. God speaks, and it is done! Hallelujah!

So shall My Word be that goes forth from My mouth; it shall not return to Me void, but it shall accomplish what I please, and it shall prosper in the thing for which I sent it. Isaiah 55:11

God's Word does not exist independently from God. Like Him, it is alive and incorruptible. It can never be destroyed or defeated because it possesses all the qualities of God Himself.

Having been born again, not of incorruptible seed but incorruptible, through the Word of God which lives and abides forever. 1 Peter 1:23

The Word is eternal because God is eternal. The Word is living because God is living. The Word is powerful because God is powerful. Everything which is true of God is also true of His Word.

This means, my friend, that you receive the very life of God when He plants the seed of His Word inside you! As you grasp God's Word, everything in His plan for your life comes within your reach.

The Word is in control

God created the heavens and the earth by the Word of His power. He spoke life and light into being

through His creative Word. He said 'Let there be', and it happened as He spoke. Today, by exactly the same power, God keeps on sustaining all things, and accomplishing His eternal will of salvation.

I am God, and there is no other; I am God, and there is none like Me, declaring the end from the beginning, and from ancient times things that are not yet done, saying, 'My counsel shall stand, and I will do all My pleasure'. Isaiah 46:9-10

First, the Father purposes His will. Then, the Word declares it - speaking out the Father's purpose. Finally, the Spirit performs the Father's will by working out every detail of His plan.

Dear friend, it is futile for people to attempt to resist God, for He always fulfils His will.

Indeed before the day was, I am He; and there is no one who can deliver out of My hand; I work, and who will reverse it? Isaiah 43:12

I'm sure you know that a wonderful Day is coming when everyone will acknowledge God's Word. Soon and very soon, every knee will bow, and every tongue confess, the glorious name of our God and Saviour, Jesus Christ! Hallelujah!

At that time, the effective operation of God's Word will be plain for all to see. But, for now, we are called to live by faith. We have the privilege of working with God as He fulfils His Word on earth.

The operation of God's Word

My friend, you must believe and act on God's Word if you want it to work effectively through you. The Word must become living and active within you if you're to become an effective instrument of God's will in your locality.

For the Word of God is living and powerful, and sharper than any two-edged sword, piercing even to the division of soul and spirit, and of joints and marrow, and is a discerner of the thoughts and intents of the heart. Hebrews 4:12

First, you must let the Word work in you by giving it access to the deepest parts of your being. This means allowing God to search your heart and to expose those things which displease Him. It's an awesome experience.

Search me, O God, and know my heart; try me and see if there is any wicked way in me; and lead me in the way everlasting. Psalm 139:23-24

When you respond to God's Word by eagerly inviting it to test your heart, the Word works even more actively within you to fulfil God's will.

Lay aside all filthiness and overflow of wickedness, and receive with meekness the implanted Word, which is able to save your souls. James 1:21

As you go on humbling yourself before the Word's infallible authority, and as you keep on submitting to its undeniable power, so God's Word goes on working in-and-through you with ever-increasing effectiveness.

Once you start to receive God's Word like this, you'll really begin to see God's promises fulfilled!

When you received the Word of God which you heard from us, you welcomed it not as the word of men, but as it is in truth, the Word of God, which also effectively works in you who believe.
1 Thessalonians 2:13

In this book, my friend, I'll show you how you to release the power of God's Word in your life.

There must be a deep work of God in your heart to start the process. The Word must grip

you in the absolute centre of your life, and you must cling to the Word with every part of your being.

As God's Word increasingly dominates your life, God will release within you all His divine capabilities.

⇒ He will fulfil His Word to you.

⇒ He will keep all the promises that He has given you.

⇒ He will accomplish His good-and-perfect will in your life.

Praise His holy name!

2

God's Word in my spirit

In the last chapter, I described the power of God's Word. It possesses all the divine capabilities of God Himself. Through the Word, you have access to God's richest blessings.

As you allow the Word to work in you, so it will mature you and accomplish all God's plans and purposes for your life. Like a seed, however, God's Word must be planted, nurtured and cultivated before its fruit becomes visible.

Good gardeners respect the seed they use. They prepare the soil thoroughly and sow the seed carefully. They then feed and water the young plant until it produces what they planned.

This is how you should handle the Word. First, you must recognise that it is the Word of God. You should respect it because you respect the One who speaks it.

On this one will I look: on him who is poor and of a contrite spirit, and who trembles at My Word. Isaiah 66:2

Dear friend, do you tremble before the Word? Do you respect God that much? Sadly, many Christians treat God's Word casually when it should be their most sacred and precious resource. We've no right to treat the Word lightly when God is so serious about it.

When we respect the Word deeply, we will approach it humbly. We'll take care that we do not read into it what God is not saying, and that we obey only what He is saying.

The seed of the Word

The human spirit is the soil into which the Word must be sown. God's words are spirit and life, and only a fool approaches God's Word with their human understanding. Instead, we must hear it, receive it, and understand it - *spiritually*.

When God speaks, His breath - His Spirit - communicates directly with our spirits. This is why we must receive the Word in our spirits.

Many people hear the Word regularly, and yet it doesn't affect them. They study the Bible, listen to sermons, read Christian books, and yet the Word produces no fruit in their lives. How can this be?

The main reason is that they don't open their spirits to receive the Word. They think about the Word with their minds, but they don't allow God to speak to them deep inside - in their spirits.

God's Word operates in-and-through people only from within human spirits which have truly welcomed and received the Word.

Your Word I have hidden in my heart that I might not sin against You. Psalm 119:11

Remember, my friend, that God always blesses a humble attitude, an eagerness to listen to Him, and a willingness to obey Him.

God's Word will prosper you

God's way leads to an abundant and fruitful life; while the path of the wicked leads to misery and hopelessness. Too many people follow either their own thoughts and inclinations, or other people's ideas and opinions.

Although the paths based on human opinions may seem attractive, they all eventually fail. Only the way which is grounded in God's Word endures.

As you learn to delight yourself in God's Word, and to follow His will, you'll find that it's the path to abundant and everlasting life.

God has a special promise for those who delight in His Word and meditate on it day and night:

He shall be like a tree planted by the rivers of water, that brings forth its fruit in its season, whose leaf also shall not wither. And whatever he does shall prosper. Psalm 1:3

Soon after Moses had died, God challenged Joshua to meditate on the Word and to obey it completely. With this divine command, however, there came an encouraging promise.

For then you will make your way prosperous, and then you will have good success. Joshua 1:8

When God's Word abides in you, it provides you with both strength and victory over the evil one. My dear friend, there's no greater defence against Satan's attacks than the Word of God. Even Jesus used the Word during His time of testing in the wilderness.

The Bible reports that Jesus used the weapon of the Word three times against the evil one. And we can overcome the devil today in exactly the same way - every time that we need to! Hallelujah!

I have written to you because you are strong, and the Word of God abides in you, and you have overcome the wicked one. 1 John 2:14

Ask what you desire

Most believers know that they can do nothing without Jesus. This is why He told us to be careful to abide in Him at all times. But do you know what this means in practice?

You may know that the Holy Spirit lives in you, but how can you be sure that you're really abiding in Christ?

Jesus provided the answer when He said, 'Abide in Me, and let My words abide in you.' Read on, dear friend, and see the astounding promise which accompanies His statement.

If you abide in Me, and My words abide in you, you will ask what you desire, and it shall be done for you. John 15:7

Can you see the enormous implications? As you let the words of Christ live in you, so His desires become your desires.

When Jesus' words are in us, they empower us to want what He wants and will what He wills. When we pray with His Word in us, we're so tuned to God's will that we don't need to pray, 'If it be Thy will'. We already know God's will because the Word in us has been shaping our deepest desires!

When you begin to understand these truths, you'll develop a deep hunger for the Word which will never leave you. You won't be able to get enough of it! You'll meditate on it day and night. You'll share the Psalmist's opinion of God's Word.

More to be desired are they than gold, yea, than much fine gold; sweeter also than honey and the honeycomb. Psalm 19:11

Now, we're going to see how the Word of God begins to operate in-and-through you to fulfil *every* promise of God in your life.

3

God's Word in my mouth

God's Word is never stale or static; it's always alive and active. When you first believe God, you begin a living relationship with the Word which then starts to work dynamically within you.

God speaks His Word into your spirit, and this conceives faith. The Spirit then keeps on feeding your faith until the Word is fulfilled and God's answer has come.

For your part, you begin by hearing the Word and receiving it, like a seed, deep into your spirit. You must then cling onto the Word by confessing it and acting on it - this develops faith. Finally, when faith has matured, God's promise comes.

Your salvation is a clear example of this process. You heard the Word of the gospel. The Spirit began to work in you, and eventually brought you to full conviction. You welcomed the good news into your spirit. Faith then began to emerge and develop until it was seen and heard in your life.

Faith's confession

Every Word from God which you truly receive in your spirit soon begins to reveal itself in your thoughts, your deeds and your words. The link between what you believe in your spirit and what you say with your mouth is called 'confession'.

In the New Testament, the Greek word for 'confession' means 'saying the same as'. Your thoughts, words and actions 'confess' the Word by thinking, saying and doing *the same* as the Word.

When we examine the faith process more closely, we can see that there is actually a *double agreement* in biblical confession.

Confession is not just saying that you agree with God's Word. It's also agreeing with what you say in the deepest part of your being. This means that it is one thing to speak God's Word with your mouth, but quite another to make a biblical confession.

The second degree of agreement means that your mouth must agree with your spirit. There's no true confession without this corresponding inner conviction.

In a true faith confession, your mouth must agree with your spirit, and your spirit must agree with God's Word. Faith operates only when your mouth, your spirit and God's Word are all in line.

For with the heart one believes unto righteousness, and with the mouth confession is made unto salvation. Romans 10:10

Can you see how your heart - the essence of your being - carries the conviction of faith, and how your mouth then lines up with this inner conviction?

This is how every true confession operates - from the beginning to the end of salvation. This vital principle applies to every promise of God.

My dear friend, you simply cannot keep God's living faith locked up inside you. If you truly believe something, if you're really full of it, you should be bursting to declare it!

Remember, Jesus taught you that your mouth is the overflow of your heart.

For out of the abundance of the heart the mouth speaks. Matthew 12:34

Whatever fills your life eventually overflows from your mouth. If you're full of love, you'll naturally speak words of love. But if you're full of secret anger, you won't be able to stop some angry words from slipping out of your mouth.

We're all influenced by the dominant force or interest in our lives - it can be money, work, sport, family, religion, and so on. This affects everything about us - including our words and deeds.

This is how faith works. If we're full of faith, words of faith are simply bound to pour from our lips. It's a basic divine principle.

God's faith covenant

God is the God of covenant. This means that God does everything by covenants. (A covenant is a legally sealed-and-binding agreement.)

When God makes a covenant, it is always consistent with *His loving nature*, for God cannot act contrary to His gracious name and nature.

God created humanity in His image and likeness, which implies that we also have a covenant nature. And so, throughout the Scriptures, we find God making covenants with people.

There are many biblical covenants, but they're all summarised within one basic covenant promise:

I will walk among you and be your God, and you shall be My people. Leviticus 26:12

The great covenant gift is God's own glorious presence. He promises us Himself! Hallelujah!

How the covenant works

The covenant which God made with us operates only through the blood of Jesus. At the last supper, Jesus took the cup and said, 'This is the new covenant in My blood.'

All the Old Testament covenants were sealed with animal blood, but Jesus' perfect blood has sealed the covenant which God has made with us.

The Father wills, initiates and seals the covenant. Our part is simply to respond with faith to His grace. As we believe God, so the covenant operates in our lives. His presence comes to us, and - with it - everything His presence provides.

By faith, we enter deeply into the marvellous presence of God. The Holy Spirit - God's covenant gift for all believers - both grants us access to God and begins to inspire us so that God's words become our words.

In an important Old Testament passage, God reveals how His covenant operates through faith.

This is My covenant with them: My Spirit who is upon you, and My words which I have put in your mouth, shall not depart from your mouth, nor from the mouth of your descendants, nor from the mouth of your descendants' descendants, from this time and for evermore. Isaiah 59:21

Can you see that God's covenant operates through confession? It works when God's Spirit is on us and His Word is in our mouth. The promises of the covenant are fulfilled when we declare them!

The Spirit of the covenant

You must realise, however, that faith-declarations can be made only in-and-with the Holy Spirit.

There are two basic Spirit-inspired declarations. In the New Testament, the Spirit prompts-and-helps us to say *'Abba, Father'* and *'Jesus is Lord'*.

Nobody can make either of these biblical declarations without the help of the Holy Spirit. It is He who bears witness with-and-to us that we are God's children. And it is He who testifies with-and-to us that Jesus is Lord.

Every blessing of God flows from, and depends on, these two confessions or declarations of faith.

In-and-with the Spirit, we first acknowledge that we are the Father's children and the objects of the Father's love and blessing. Then we understand that it is all made possible only by the power and authority of the Ruler over all - Jesus Christ!

Three further biblical faith-declarations or confessions are associated with the new covenant:

⇒ '*Amen*' is the Spirit-inspired agreement to the truth of God's Word;

⇒ '*Hallelujah*' is the highest form of Spirit-directed joy;

⇒ '*Maranatha*' is the witness we share with the Spirit to the hope of Jesus' return.

We can then add to these biblical faith-declarations every Spirit-inspired utterance which is in line with God's Word.

My friend, as you welcome God's Word into your spirit, and as you allow it to work in you, so faith will well up inside you. Make sure that you express this faith in Spirit-directed declarations of praise, hope and confidence in God.

Meditate on God's Word. Feed your faith daily. Express it in obedient actions. Make frequent, jubilant declarations of faith. And wait patiently for God's Word to be fulfilled in your life.

How to use Part Two

In Part Two, I'm going to show you many of the most important blessings and promises of the new covenant. As you read through these pages, prepare for a faith explosion!

There are *three* sections in each chapter.

First, I'll give you a short description of the blessing. Please read this section carefully. Make sure that you understand it completely. And ask God to show you how to apply it in your life and situation.

Then, I'll provide you with many scriptural verses about the blessing. Study them slowly. Read them several times. Return to them whenever you have a related need. A few verses are highlighted by a box - these are for you to memorise. Let God's Spirit impregnate your spirit with the seed of His Word!

Finally, I'll suggest a *faith declaration* for you to make. Read this through silently several times to ensure that your spirit agrees with God's Word. Then make the declaration *aloud* - you're proclaiming your faith to God, to yourself, and to the principalities and powers of the heavenly realm.

If you find it helpful, you can adapt the declarations to suit your situation by specifying the details of your circumstances. You can even make the declarations in a group with other believers by changing 'I' to 'we'.

You'll probably find it useful to return frequently to these declarations in the future. As you confess God's Word with sincerity, you'll find that His Word will develop your faith, defeat your enemy, and deliver God's promises. Hallelujah!

Don't try to read all the chapters in Part Two at one sitting. You'll get far more benefit if you take one chapter a day as a special devotion. May God bless you as you begin your adventure of faith!

Part Two

GOD'S BLESSINGS

4

New Creation

In the beginning, God created the heavens and the earth by the Word of His power. He filled the universe with His beauty, His joy and His glory.

As a special act of love, God made humanity in His own personal image. Adam and Eve were the crowning act of creation, and they were blessed with a special place on earth in the garden of Eden.

God's plan was for *all people* to live with Him for ever, like Adam and Eve, in perfect fellowship!

But they disobeyed God, and the beauty of God's handiwork was spoilt by their sin. As a result, Adam and Eve were expelled from Eden, humanity was banished from God's presence, and every part of creation came under God's curse.

Sin began to spread and take effect. Everything was subjected to futility. Sickness, pain and death polluted every part of God's world.

The God of hope

But God did not abandon His world or the people He'd made. When He pronounced His curse, He offered the first promise of salvation - a promise which pointed to Jesus.

God promised that the woman's seed would crush the serpent's head, and that the serpent would bruise the seed's heel. This was fulfilled when Jesus died on the cross and destroyed Satan's kingdom.

On the cross, Jesus paid the price of sin and released God's new creation power. Calvary marks the end of the old and the beginning of the new.

The new creation has begun. In His resurrection, Jesus became the 'first-fruit' of the new creation - which will come in its fullness when Jesus returns.

The resurrection from the dead and the redemption of the body are our great hope. When

Jesus comes again, we'll never have to face pain, sickness, sin, temptation, weakness, failure, death - or anything which has to do with the old life.

Yet this new creation has already begun. Old things *have* passed away; all things *have* become new. People who are in Christ Jesus are participating *now* in God's new creation.

My friend, if you're a believer, you are in Christ; and the Bible promises that you already have:

⇒ *a new standing with God* - you've been justified, declared righteous by faith;

⇒ *a new relationship with God* - you've been adopted as God's child, born into His family;

⇒ *a new fellowship with the Holy Spirit* - you've been indwelt and filled by the Spirit;

⇒ *a new life of freedom* - you've been set free from the power of sin, death and the devil;

⇒ *a new position* - you've been seated with Christ in heavenly places;

⇒ *a new destiny* - you've been promised a great inheritance as a joint-heir with Christ;

⇒ *a new security* - your old life has gone forever, and now you are hidden in Christ.

Praise God, these promises are true and glorious!

God's words for you

If anyone is in Christ, he is a new creation; old things have passed away; behold all things have become new.
2 Corinthians 5:17

The earnest expectation of the creation eagerly waits for the revealing of the sons of God *Romans 8:19*

Creation itself also will be delivered from the bondage of corruption into the glorious liberty of the children of God.
Romans 8:21

We also who have the first-fruits of the Spirit, even we groan within ourselves, eagerly waiting for the adoption, the redemption of our body. *Romans 8:23*

Blessed be the God and Father of our Lord Jesus Christ, who according to His abundant mercy has begotten us again to a living hope through the resurrection of Jesus Christ from the dead. *1 Peter 1:3*

Having been justified by faith, we have peace with God through our Lord Jesus Christ. *Romans 5:1*

God predestined us to adoption as sons by Jesus Christ to Himself, according to the good pleasure of His will.
Ephesians 1:5

Having been born again, not of corruptible seed but incorruptible, through the Word of God which lives and abides for ever. *1 Peter 1:23*

You are not in the flesh but in the Spirit, if indeed the Spirit of God dwells in you. *Romans 8:9*

He who hears My word and believes in Him who sent Me has everlasting life, and shall not come to judgement, but has passed from death into life. *John 5:24*

Through death, He might destroy him who had the power of death, that is, the devil, and release those who through fear of death were all their lifetime subject to bondage. *Hebrews 2:14-15*

You are of God, and have overcome, because He who is in you is greater than he who is in the world. *1 John 4:4*

You know Him who is from the beginning, and you are strong, and the Word of God abides in you, and you have overcome the wicked one. *1 John 1:14*

The Spirit himself bears witness with our spirit that we are children of God, and if children, then heirs - heirs of God and joint heirs with Christ. *Romans 8:16-17*

God, who is rich in mercy, because of His great love with which He loved us, even when we were dead in trespasses, made us alive together with Christ. *Ephesians 2:4-5*

You died, and your life is hidden with Christ in God. When Christ who is our life appears, then you also will appear with Him in glory. *Colossians 3:3-4*

Those whom He foreknew, He also predestined to be conformed to the image of His Son, that He might be the first-born among many brethren. Moreover, whom he predestined, these he also called; whom He called, these He also justified; and whom he justified, these He also glorified. *Romans 8:29-30*

Your faith declaration

"I confess and declare that I am a new creation in Christ. My old things have passed away, and my life has been made new.

I now walk in the power of Almighty God's new creation, with my eyes fixed firmly on the hope of my calling.

I am being renewed every day by the Holy Spirit, who lives in me and fills me with God's wonderful presence and power.

The Father has declared me righteous. He has adopted me into His family. And He has set me free from the power of sin, death and the devil.

I am now seated with Christ in heavenly places. I am a co-heir with Christ and an inheritor of the kingdom of heaven.

I have been crucified with Christ, and my life is now hidden with Him in God, my Father.

I now live my life in the body by the faith of Jesus, who saves me by His grace.

My new creation passion is to live for my Lord and my God, and to love and enjoy Him for ever."

5

Forgiveness

God's gift of forgiveness must be the best news in the Bible! It meets your most basic need as a sinner and establishes your relationship with God forever.

Without forgiveness you could never have any lasting joy, or peace, or hope. With forgiveness, however, you can say goodbye to all your guilt and shame and fear.

Because God is the eternal Creator, He's the holy and righteous judge of the whole earth. As the moral ruler of all humanity, He must ensure that all sin is justly punished. This means that everyone should be condemned to eternal abandonment.

Nobody has any hope of standing before God in their own goodness, because no one can perfectly fulfil God's righteous standards.

God, however, longs to re-establish the loving relationship with His creation that He enjoyed before the Fall. He aches to forgive the sins of the world, and so to be reconciled with humanity. But how can a righteous God do this?

He cannot ignore our sin, because this would make Him unjust. But if He judged our sin justly, we would all be separated from Him for ever.

The good news of God's gracious and merciful forgiveness is that He's found a solution! He has reached into His own loving nature and found a way of being *both* the righteous Judge of the universe *and* the Saviour of the world.

The solution is the cross. The Father sent His only Son into His fallen world to live a perfect life *and* to die a sinner's death.

When Jesus died on the cross, God dealt with *all* the sin of the *whole* world. This means that you're no longer condemned by God because of your sin.

My friend, this is the wonderful gift of forgiveness that you received when you believed in Jesus. Hallelujah!

Righteous by faith

The Father's act of forgiveness involves more than the removal of your past sins. It also provides you with a right standing before Him. By faith, you've been declared *righteous*. This is what it means to be 'justified' - to be 'just-as-if-I'd never sinned'.

This is all God's work of grace. It has nothing to do with anything you've ever done, or could ever do, to make yourself right with God.

The Father's overflowing goodness and mercy in Christ means that all your sins are gone for ever – past, present *and* future!

I'm sure some of you are wondering how this can be. The answer, my friend, lies in appreciating what Jesus' death has actually achieved for you, as a believer.

Jesus lived the life that you should have lived, and then He died the death you deserve to die. He lived a perfect life, but died the worst of sinners.

He died the death that you should die so that you can receive the life that you should live. As a result, by faith, you now stand righteous before the Father - it's as if you'd never sinned! Hallelujah!

Of course, you should continue to confess your sins and seek God's on-going forgiveness; and you should respond to His forgiveness by forgiving others. But, now, your new relationship with the Father can never be broken. Your forgiveness is an unchangeable, unbreakable, eternal fact.

⇒ You've been forgiven - once-and-for-all.

⇒ God is now your very own merciful Father.

⇒ You'll never stand before Him as a sinner before a Judge.

⇒ He has removed your guilt, your sin and your condemnation *for ever*!

Praise His holy name and nature!

God's words for you

Blessed is he whose transgression is forgiven, whose sin is covered. Blessed is the man to whom the Lord does not impute iniquity, and in whose spirit there is no deceit.

Psalm 32:1-2

I, even I, am He who blots out your transgressions for My own sake; and I will not remember your sin. *Isaiah 43:25*

If anyone sins, we have an Advocate with the Father, Jesus Christ the righteous. And He Himself is the propitiation for our sins, and not for ours only but also for the whole world. *1 John 2:1-2*

Bless the Lord, O my soul, and forget not all His benefits: Who forgives all your iniquities, who heals all your diseases. *Psalm 103:1-3*

There is therefore now no condemnation to those who are in Christ Jesus, who do not walk according to the flesh, but according to the Spirit. *Romans 8:1*

As the heavens are high above the earth, so great is His mercy toward those who fear Him; as far as the east is from the west, so far has He removed our transgressions from us. *Psalm 103:11-12*

If You, Lord, should mark iniquities, who could stand? But there is forgiveness with You, that You may be feared. *Psalm 130:3-4*

Therefore, having been justified by faith, we have peace with God through our Lord Jesus Christ. *Romans 5:1*

If we walk in the light as He is in the light, we have fellowship with one another, and the blood of Jesus Christ His Son cleanses us from all sin. *1 John 1:7*

If we confess our sins, He is faithful and just to forgive us our sins and to cleanse us from all unrighteousness. *1 John 1:9*

To him who does not work but believes on Him who justifies the ungodly, his faith is accounted for righteousness. *Romans 4:5*

For He made Him who knew no sin to be sin for us, that we might become the righteousness of God in Him. *2 Corinthians 5:21*

Your faith declaration

"I confess and declare that I'm righteous, clean and whole in the presence of my heavenly Father.

I walk in the light of God's Word; and the blood of Jesus, God's only Son, cleanses me from all sin.

I know that the forgiveness which God has given me is total, unconditional and permanent. I will never come under His condemnation again, for Christ Himself is my full justification.

On the cross, Jesus died my death that I might live His life. He took my sin that I might share His righteousness. I am ever-loved and fully-accepted by God, in Christ Jesus.

I declare that no demon, no principality, no evil power - not even the devil himself - can ever bring any charge against me. Hallelujah!

My personal unworthiness has been lost for ever in the infinite sea of God's love. My sin, my guilt and my shame have vanished for all eternity. Nothing can bring them back.

And now, the sole aim of my life is to please the One who saved me. I live in the Spirit of His grace, and walk in the forgiveness of God."

6

Assurance

My dear friend, God wants you to be 100% sure of your full salvation. He doesn't want you to have *any doubts* about the matter at all.

In Christ, the Father has dealt decisively with all your sin and guilt. And, in the Spirit, He's given you the holy boldness you need to live in His presence. What more can He do to convince you?

What a pity, then, that some Christians continue to live as though they were still sinners under the enemy's condemnation; and that other Christians have so little confidence in the Father's love.

Too many believers seem to think that they must hide behind the love of Jesus to be saved from the only-just-contained wrath of a still-angry Father. They do not revel in their wonderful status as sons and daughters of the Father.

But God wants you to live in the fullness of the joy of your total salvation. The Father's perfect love is able to drive away every tormenting fear that you have. You can live above your doubts and rise in the full assurance of your faith.

Remember, my friend, the cross has not prompted the Father to love you a little bit more - for He always has loved you with infinite love. Nor has the cross turned God into a Father - for He's been the Father throughout all eternity.

Rather, the cross has made it possible for the Father to treat sinners as sons and daughters. This is a caste-iron, indisputable fact; and, for this, you should give Him unceasing praise and thanks.

Some people can accept that God *has saved* them, but they are not sure of His power *to keep them saved.* They're frightened that they might be lost in the end.

But Jesus is the author *and* the finisher of your faith. What He starts, He always completes.

Dear friend, the Father loves you with an everlasting love, and nothing will ever separate you from Him. The blood of Jesus eternally seals and guarantees His love for you. The name of Jesus is your eternal protection, and you are safe in Him.

God's purpose for you is that you'll enjoy a kingdom which will last for ever. Even now, you are seated with Christ in heavenly places. You're already glorified through faith in Christ!

So get rid of all your foolish, guilty fears. Release them today! Rest in the Father's saving-and-keeping power. Let the fact of the cross be your daily assurance as you enjoy the full salvation that God has graciously given you.

God's words for you

I am not ashamed, for I know whom I have believed and am persuaded that He is able to keep what I have committed to Him until that Day. *2 Timothy 1:12*

These things I have written to you who believe in the name of the Son of God, that you may know that you have eternal life, and that you may continue to believe in the name of the Son of God. *1 John 5:13*

Being confident of this very thing, that He who has begun a good work in you will complete it until the day of Jesus Christ. *Philippians 1:6*

For I am persuaded that neither death nor life, nor angels nor principalities nor powers, nor things present nor things to come, nor height nor depth, nor any other created thing, shall be able to separate us from the love of God which is in Christ Jesus our Lord. *Romans 8:38-39*

Now to Him who is able to keep you from stumbling, and to present you faultless before the presence of His glory with exceeding joy. *Jude 1:24*

Most assuredly, I say to you, he who hears My word and believes in Him who sent Me has everlasting life, and shall not come into judgement, but has passed from death into life. *John 5:24*

I give them eternal life, and they shall never perish; neither shall anyone snatch them out of My hand. My Father, who has given them to Me, is greater than all; and no one is able to snatch them out of My Father's hand. *John 10:27-29*

For I know the thoughts that I think toward you, says the Lord, thoughts of peace and not of evil, to give you a future and a hope. *Jeremiah 29:11*

The eternal God is your refuge, and underneath are the everlasting arms; he will thrust out the enemy from before you, and will say, 'Destroy!' *Deuteronomy 33:27*

Let us run with endurance the race that is set before us, looking unto Jesus, the author and finisher of our faith, who for the joy that was set before Him endured the cross, despising the shame, and has sat down at the right hand of the throne of God. *Hebrews 12:1-2*

The Lord has appeared of old to me, saying, 'Yes, I have loved you with an everlasting love; therefore with loving-kindness I have drawn you'. *Jeremiah 31:3*

Let your conduct be without covetousness; be content with such things as you have. For He Himself has said, 'I will never leave you nor forsake you.' *Hebrews 13:5*

For whom He foreknew, He also predestined to be conformed to the image of His Son, that He might be the firstborn among many brethren. *Romans 8:29*

This is the will of the Father who sent Me, that of all He has given Me I should lose nothing, but should raise it up at the last day. *John 6:39*

Who shall bring a charge against God's elect? It is God who justifies. Who is he who condemns? It is Christ who died, and furthermore is also risen, who is even at the right hand of God, who also makes intercession for us. *Romans 8:33-34*

For you died, and your life is hidden with Christ in God. When Christ who is our life appears, then you also will appear with Him in glory. *Colossians 3:3-4*

Now may the God of peace Himself sanctify you completely; and may your whole spirit, soul, and body be preserved blameless at the coming of our Lord Jesus Christ. He who calls you is faithful, who also will do it. *1Thessalonians 5:23-24*

Father, keep through Your name those whom You have given Me, that they may be one as We are. *John 17:11*

Your faith declaration

"I confess and declare that my joy and salvation are fully complete in Christ Jesus.

He is the Author, and the Finisher, of my personal faith. And He will bring to perfection the good work that He's already begun in my life.

I have passed from death to life, from despair to hope, from tears to joy, and I have become the Father's beloved child forever.

I know that no power in heaven, or on earth, or under the earth, can ever separate me from the Father's goodness and love.

I declare that the precious blood of Jesus guarantees the Father's love to me; and that the rugged cross of Calvary is my daily assurance of salvation.

I am now seated with Christ in heavenly places. And I live in the enjoyment of the full salvation which the Father has so graciously given me.

God, my Father, is faithful, and I put my trust in His power to save me, and to keep me, until the coming Day of Christ."

7

Freedom

Genuine freedom is found only in Jesus. He wasn't exaggerating when He said, 'If the Son sets you free, you shall be free indeed!'

But, my friend, you can experience and enjoy Christ's freedom only when you *know* about it. Too many believers still live like prisoners because they haven't realised that they've been released.

The Spirit wants to give you a precious revelation about your true position in-and-through Christ.

The Father created you to be entirely free, and your present position in Christ is the highest possible expression of this total freedom.

The New Testament uses a word from first-century slave markets to describe your freedom in Christ. In those days, slaves could become free men and women only when they were 'redeemed' by the payment of the prescribed price.

In the same way, Christ has paid the full price for your total-and-permanent 'redemption' from the guilt and power of sin. And, one day, you'll be redeemed from sin's effects in your physical body.

In your old life, you were controlled by Satan, and by the law of sin and death which worked in you. You were a slave to the sins and habits of the flesh.

You might have been able to make the conditions of slavery a little bit easier, but there was nothing you could do to release yourself from slavery.

But now you've been released in-and-by Christ. He has presented the only acceptable price for your total freedom - His perfect blood. Hallelujah!

This means, my friend, that you've been released from *all* the things which once held you captive.

By His death, Jesus has destroyed all those forces which once gripped and controlled you, and has given you a new life of unconditional freedom for you to enjoy with Him for ever.

Deliverance by death

By faith, Jesus' death becomes your death, so that His life can be your life. This means that, in Christ, you're now dead to sin and alive to God. You can enjoy your new life of freedom in the Spirit!

On the cross, Christ redeemed you from the curse of the law and broke the power of sin in your life. Condemnation is gone! Sin has lost its grip! You've died with Christ and have been raised with Him into His resurrection life of victory.

Christ Himself is now your life, and He lives His life in you through the enabling of the Holy Spirit. This means that you can live as Jesus lives – beyond the control of Satan's power.

Of course, your freedom in Christ is useless in your practical, day-to-day life *unless* you continue to depend on Him completely, and to draw from His power at work in you.

You must walk by obedient faith, dear friend, and keep on putting to death the things which belong to your former manner of living.

You'll live the resurrection life of the Spirit only as you believe, confess and act on the Word which tells you of your freedom. Without this holy, Spirit-inspired confidence, you will tend to stay locked inside the prison of your former self.

Stand up, my friend, and look around. You're totally free in Christ! The prison doors are open! The chains of slavery, which once bound you, have been unlocked and thrown away for ever!

Don't let the devil's lies hold you back for one moment longer! Stand up in your freedom! Walk away from your habits, and live the life of victory!

God's words for you

You shall know the truth, and the truth shall make you free. *John 8:32*

Because of the blood of your covenant, I will set your prisoners free from the waterless pit. *Zechariah 9:11*

Knowing this, that our old man was crucified with Him, that the body of sin might be done away with, that we should no longer be slaves of sin. *Romans 6:6*

If the Son makes you free, you shall be free indeed. *John 8:36*

Likewise you also, reckon yourselves to be dead indeed to sin, but alive to God in Christ Jesus our Lord. *Romans 6:11*

Having been set free from sin, you became slaves of righteousness. *Romans 6:18*

The captives of the mighty shall be taken away, and the prey of the terrible be delivered; for I will contend with him and save your children. *Isaiah 49:25*

Take My yoke upon you and learn from Me, for I am gentle and lowly in heart, and you will find rest for your souls. For My yoke is easy and My burden is light. *Matthew 11:29-30*

You have broken the yoke of his burden and the staff of his shoulder, the rod of his oppressor, as in the day of Midian. *Isaiah 9:4*

The Spirit of the Lord is upon Me, because He has anointed Me to preach the gospel to the poor; He has sent Me to heal the broken-hearted, to proclaim liberty to the captives and recovery of sight to the blind, to set at liberty those who are oppressed. *Luke 4:18*

Stand fast therefore in the liberty by which Christ has made us free, and do not be entangled again with a yoke of bondage. *Galatians 5:1*

He who sins is of the devil, for the devil has sinned from the beginning. For this purpose the Son of God was manifested, that He might destroy the works of the devil. *1 John 3:8*

Whoever has been born of God does not sin, for His seed remains in him; and he cannot sin, because he has been born of God. *1 John 3:9*

For the law of the Spirit of life in Christ Jesus has made me free from the law of sin and death. *Romans 8:2*

Your faith declaration

"I confess and declare that I know and enjoy the absolute freedom of God. Jesus Christ has set me free from the guilt and power of sin! And I am free indeed!

I have been crucified with Christ, and have been raised into His resurrection life of perfect liberty.

I know that the Son of God was manifested with the purpose of destroying all the evil works of the enemy. And I know that He has done this in me.

I walk in the freedom of the Spirit, and have been liberated by the law of love. I have been delivered from the curse of the Law, and I am no longer bound by sin, or by the flesh, or by the devil.

I announce that I am now free to do right, to obey God's will, and to serve my Lord and Saviour with every part of my being.

I know that I'm not my own, for I was bought by a great and blood-stained price. I now belong to Jesus, and am eager do His bidding.

I renounce sin, Satan, and all his evil, selfish works. I stand firm in my freedom, and live in the victory of Christ forever."

8

The Lordship of Jesus

The Lordship of Jesus Christ is one of the most important Christian truths. In fact, my friend, your entire life of faith depends on it.

Your faith is empty, and you have no hope of salvation, if Jesus is not *the Lord* (the ultimate authority in creation, the absolute ruler of the universe), and if He has not proved His Lordship by rising from the dead.

But:

⇒ Jesus *is* alive;

⇒ He *is* Lord;

⇒ And you *are* saved. *Hallelujah!*

The Name above all names

The Bible states that the Father has rewarded Jesus with a special name.

Jesus is the eternal Son of the eternal Father. As the Son, He shares the same divine nature as the Father and the Spirit. Why, then, does the Father give the Son the special name, *'The LORD'*?

In the beginning, God demonstrated His Lordship by His kingly rule throughout heaven and earth.

But Lucifer, a senior angel, defied God's rule and wanted to replace Him. Because of his rebellious ambition, Lucifer became Satan - the adversary - and was banished from heaven.

Satan's rebellion soon spread to earth, as Adam and Eve disobeyed God's rule. In this way, Satan established an illegal 'kingdom' where he ruled.

But his rebel kingdom was doomed from the start, and the merciful Father mounted a mighty rescue mission. He sent the Son to earth to win back all those who were held captive in Satan's kingdom of sin, sickness, misery, fear and death.

Jesus came and fulfilled the Father's conditions of right living. Finally, He died as the once-and-for-all substitute sacrifice for the sin of all humanity.

At the cross, God personally paid the full price of all our rebellious disobedience. The Father suffered the infinite grief of love, and the Son endured the Father's abandonment - because of our sin.

Setting the hostages free

It was a heroic rescue. Jesus entered Satan's realm, bound the strong man, and set the captives free.

By His deeds, Jesus was qualified to be the leader of a new, rescued humanity. He died and rose again to represent us as our risen, triumphant ruler.

It was at this point that God named Jesus as '*LORD*'. In effect, the Father handed the executive authority of the universe to the Son.

All authority is now in the Son's hands. This means that Jesus is Lord and that Satan is defeated, disarmed and driven out - all by Christ's victory.

And, today, the Lord Jesus rules and reigns from heaven's high throne – the executive seat of the universe – at the right hand of the Father.

Jesus' Lordship is not something to consider just as some kind of theological statement. Instead, it's a cause for tremendous praise! It means that the battle is over. The kingdom of God has triumphed!

Jesus' Lordship calls for your total surrender and absolute obedience. How can we call Him 'Lord' unless we obey Him and submit to His authority?

Wonderfully, this authority has now become *your* authority. You're called, my friend, to go in Jesus' name and to do the works of His kingdom. He said 'Go into all the world, and preach the gospel. Heal the sick and raise the dead!' This is your mission!

As you submit to Jesus' Lordship *in* your life, His authority will become evident *through* your life. This is how you can clearly demonstrate God's kingdom throughout your part of the world.

God's words for you

He humbled Himself and became obedient to the point of death, even the death of the cross. Therefore God also has highly exalted Him and given Him the name which is above every name *Philippians 2:8-9*

At the name of Jesus every knee should bow, of those in heaven, and of those on earth, and of those under the earth, and every tongue should confess that Jesus Christ is Lord, to the glory of God the Father. *Philippians 2:10-11*

He raised Him from the dead and seated Him at His right hand in the heavenly places, far above all principality and power and might and dominion, and every name that is named, not only in this age but also in that which is to come. *Ephesians 1:20-21*

We see Jesus, who was made a little lower than the angels, for the suffering of death crowned with glory and honour, that He, by the grace of God, might taste death for everyone. *Hebrews 2:9*

I am He who lives, and was dead, and behold, I am alive forevermore. Amen. And I have the keys of Hades and of Death. *Revelation 1:18*

In as much then as the children have partaken of flesh and blood, He Himself likewise shared in the same, that through death He might destroy him who had the power of death, that is, the devil. *Hebrews 2:14*

Having wiped out the handwriting of requirements that was against us... And He has taken it out of the way, having nailed it to the cross. Having disarmed principalities and powers, He made a public spectacle of them, triumphing over them. *Colossians 2:14-15*

Now is the judgement of this world; now the ruler of this world will be cast out. *John 12:31*

Being the brightness of His glory and the image of His person, and upholding all things by the Word of His power, when He had purged our sins, sat down at the right hand of the Majesty on high. *Hebrews 1:3*

Jesus came and spoke to them, saying, 'All authority has been given to Me in heaven and on earth'. *Matthew 28:18*

Go therefore and make disciples of all the nations, baptising them in the name of the Father and of the Son and of the Holy Spirit, teaching them to observe all things that I have commanded you; and lo, I am with you always, even to the end of the age. *Matthew 28:19-20*

Your faith declaration

"I confess and declare that Jesus Christ is Lord of lords, and I glorify Him as my God and my King. He reigns supreme over all things, and I willingly submit to His authority and power.

Jesus is my Head, and the only sovereign Lord of my life. I have no other god but Him, and I yield to no other power than His.

Jesus is Lord over my spirit, and no other spirit can lord it over me.

I surrender every thought, every word, and every deed, to the Lordship of Jesus. I acknowledge that all my circumstances are under His sovereign control. Nothing can ever happen to me without His permission.

I take the name of Jesus as my authority over my world. In the mighty name of Jesus, I stand firm against every opposing spirit.

I now fill my mouth with bold praise, and I loudly confess the Lordship of Jesus.

The resurrected Lord of glory is with me at all times, and I shall never be moved. Praise His holy name!"

9

The blood

The blood-stained cross of Jesus stands at the very centre of Christianity. In all ages, throughout all traditions, on every continent, His cross has been continuously recognised as the universal symbol of our faith.

In times past, the content of hymns, the shape of buildings, the decorations on windows, the ornaments in churches, the emblem around necks, all illustrated the absolute centrality of the cross.

Without it, there would be no salvation. Quite simply, it's the red blood on the rugged cross which has opened the way for you to enter into the royal presence of the righteous God.

Jesus' blood on the cross has earnt your peace, your reconciliation with God, your redemption from sin, and your righteousness before the Father.

His blood has cleansed you from sin; removed the Father's wrath; released you from the devil, death and guilt; and removed every obstacle between you and God.

The blood has defeated Satan, and it still drives him away from your life. When Jesus died on the cross, He destroyed every negative thing which binds you to the devil. There's nothing left for Satan to use against you before God!

Some believers talk much about 'pleading the blood'. The truth, my friend, is that you don't have to plead the blood; instead, *it is the blood of Christ which pleads for you!*

The blood speaks

The book of Genesis describes Abel's murder by his brother Cain. It reports that Abel's blood cried from the ground for vengeance.

In the same way, Jesus' blood cries from heaven for mercy - upon all those who come to God through faith in the holy blood-stained cross!

Jesus' blood is the basis of His intercession with the Father. Your heavenly High Priest lives at God's right hand to intercede continuously for you.

When He died on the cross, Jesus declared 'It's finished'. This wasn't a cry of hopeless despair; it was a shout of exultant triumph. 'I've done it,' He cried, 'It's over!' 'The price has been paid and everything has been accomplished!'

Now, my friend, Jesus is in the Father's presence praying for you! He's interceding that you will:

⇒ endure to the end,

⇒ overcome in His strength,

⇒ speak His words and do His deeds,

⇒ be His nail-scarred body in your locality.

Receive fresh grace for your life from Him today!

God's words for you

They overcame him by the blood of the Lamb and by the word of their testimony, and they did not love their lives to the death. *Revelation 12:11*

The blood shall be a sign for you on the houses where you are. And when I see the blood, I will pass over you; and the plague shall not be on you to destroy you when I strike the land of Egypt. *Exodus 12:13*

The life of the flesh is in the blood, and I have given it to you upon the altar to make atonement for your souls; for it is the blood that makes atonement for the soul.

Leviticus 17:11

Being justified freely by His grace through the redemption that is in Christ Jesus, whom God set forth as a propitiation by His blood, through faith, to demonstrate His righteousness. *Romans 3:24-25*

To Jesus the Mediator of the new covenant, and to the blood of sprinkling that speaks better things than that of Abel. *Hebrews 12:24*

Not with the blood of goats and calves, but with His own blood He entered the Most Holy Place once for all, having obtained eternal redemption. *Hebrews 9:11*

In Him we have redemption through His blood, the forgiveness of sins, according to the riches of His grace.

Ephesians 1:7

If the blood of bulls and goats and the ashes of a heifer, sprinkling the unclean, sanctifies for the purifying of the flesh, how much more shall the blood of Christ, who through the eternal Spirit offered Himself without spot to God, cleanse your conscience from dead works to serve the living God? *Hebrews 9:12-14*

The blood of Jesus Christ His Son cleanses us from all sin. If we confess our sins, He is faithful and just to forgive us our sins and to cleanse us from all unrighteousness.

1 John 1:7-9

Much more then, having now been justified by His blood, we shall be saved from wrath through Him. *Romans 5:9*

Therefore Jesus also, that He might sanctify the people with His own blood, suffered outside the gate.

Hebrews 13:12

You were not redeemed with corruptible things, like silver or gold, from your aimless conduct received by tradition from your fathers, but with the precious blood of Christ, as of a lamb without blemish and without spot.

1 Peter 1:18-19

By that will we have been sanctified through the offering of the body of Jesus Christ once for all. *Hebrews 10:10*

Do you not know that your body is the temple of the Holy Spirit who is in you, whom you have from God, and you are not your own? For you were bought at a price; therefore glorify God in your body and in your spirit, which are God's. *1 Corinthians 6:19-20*

Christ has redeemed us from the curse of the law, having become a curse for us (for it is written, 'Cursed is everyone who hangs on a tree'). *Galatians 3:13*

According to the law almost all things are purified with blood, and without shedding of blood there is no remission. *Hebrews 9:22*

He then would have had to suffer often since the foundation of the world; but now, once at the end of the ages, He has appeared to put away sin by the sacrifice of Himself. *Hebrews 9:26*

Your faith declaration

"I confess and declare that I stand in the presence of God by the precious blood of Jesus. And I thank the Father for this new and living way of access into His goodness and blessing.

The blood pleads before the throne, beseeching the Father to have mercy on me.

The sacrificial death of Jesus has cleansed me from sin. It has turned away the Father's wrath. It has released me from the devil. And it has cleared every obstacle between me and God.

The blood now brings to my life all the merciful provision of the Father's great goodness.

By the blood, I stand against Satan and overcome His evil work. The blood is my security and my protection. It is my pledge and my guarantee.

I declare that the blood of the new covenant seals every promise of God to my life. It binds God to keep all His promises to me, and His Word can never be broken.

I know that the blood will never lose its power, and I rejoice in Jesus my Redeemer."

10

The Bible

God is not silent, sullen or remote; He's the God of revelation who personally speaks and declares Himself to the whole world.

Whenever God speaks, He reveals something about His own character and integrity. It is impossible for Him to lie, or to mislead, or to exaggerate, or to be 'economical with the truth'.

He is Himself 'the truth'. All His words, therefore, are both fully true and a reliable revelation of God's truth.

The Bible is 'the' written record of God's Word to humanity; it's the eternal Word expressed in a temporal form. But it doesn't contain everything that God has ever said to His people.

Rather, the Scriptures are a revelation of-and-from the Word. They are, however, a full-and-sufficient record of everything that you need for your spiritual instruction and knowledge.

Because the Bible is finite, it cannot reveal everything about the infinite God, nor can it teach you everything about eternal salvation.

But it does reveal all that you need to know about God. And it does teach all that you need to know to be saved by God and to live with-and-for God.

The New Testament states that all Scripture is 'expired' by God - that it's breathed-out by God. This shows that the Bible comes to us in exactly the same way as the Word - on God's breath.

This means that the Bible is the essential element within the Word. Every thought or idea that people claim as God's Word must be in tune with the Scriptures - for no genuine message from God could ever be inconsistent with the Bible.

God breathed the Bible to help you discover who He is, and to equip you practically for your daily life in Christ. Whatever you need to know about living with-and-for God is found in the Scriptures.

It is God's manual for life and living. If you build your life on the Bible you'll never be disappointed.

The integrity of God's Word

As the Bible comes to us on God's breath, it must be true and trustworthy. It's fully inspired, and is the very Word of God.

Although God used people to write the Bible, they wrote as they were inspired by the Holy Spirit. As a result, they wrote what God intended.

Jesus had unshakeable confidence in the Scriptures, and said that they could not be broken. He based His life and ministry on them, and used them to defeat Satan.

This means that you can trust the Bible completely. You can be certain that what God breathes in the Scriptures is 100% true.

Popular opinion may often disagree with scriptural principles, but you must put the Bible before everything else.

Your confidence in the Scriptures will be richly rewarded, for the Word cannot fail. God sends His commands to the earth, and His Word runs swiftly. God always watches over His Word to perform it.

God's words for you

By the Word of the Lord the heavens were made, and all the host of them by the breath of His mouth. *Psalm 33:6*

No prophecy of Scripture is of any private interpretation, for prophecy never came by the will of man, but holy men of God spoke as they were moved by the Holy Spirit. *2 Peter 1:20-21*

The words of the Lord are pure words, like silver tried in a furnace of earth, purified seven times. *Psalm 12:6*

As for God, His way is perfect; the Word of the Lord is proven; He is a shield to all who trust in Him. *Psalm 18:30*

It is impossible for God to lie. *Hebrews 6:18*

All Scripture is given by inspiration of God, and is profitable for doctrine, for reproof, for correction, for instruction in righteousness, that the man of God may be complete, thoroughly equipped for every good work. *2 Timothy 3:16-17*

Forever, O Lord, Your Word is settled in heaven. *Psalm 119:89*

Having been born again, not of corruptible seed but incorruptible, through the Word of God which lives and abides forever. *1 Peter 1:23*

The Scripture cannot be broken. *John 10:35*

The entirety of Your Word is truth, and every one of Your righteous judgements endures forever. *Psalm 119:160*

Heaven and earth will pass away, but My words will by no means pass away. *Luke 21:33*

The Word of our God stands for ever. *Isaiah 40:8*

There is no God in heaven or on earth like You, who keep Your covenant and mercy with Your servants who walk before you with all their hearts. You have kept what You promised; You have both spoken with Your mouth and fulfilled it with Your hand. *2 Chronicles 6:14-15*

He spoke, and it was done; He commanded, and it stood fast. *Psalm 33:9*

I am ready to perform My Word. *Jeremiah 1:12*

He sends out His command to the earth; His Word runs very swiftly. *Psalm 147:15*

The Word of God is living and powerful, and sharper than any two-edged sword, piercing even to the division of soul and spirit, and of joints and marrow, and is a discerner of the thoughts and intents of the heart. *Hebrews 4:12*

It is the Spirit who gives life; the flesh profits nothing. The words that I speak to you are spirit, and they are life. *John 6:63*

So shall My Word be that goes forth from My mouth; it shall not return to Me void, but it shall accomplish what I please, and it shall prosper in the thing for which I sent it. *Isaiah 55:11*

Whatever I command you, be careful to observe it; you shall not add to it or take away from it. *Deuteronomy 12:32*

Your faith declaration

"I confess and declare that the Bible is the written Word of God. It is inspired, infallible, authoritative, and the final authority in all things.

God's Word is alive and powerful. It is sharper than any two-edged sword, and it exposes my most secret thoughts and intentions.

I open myself to the Bible. I invite God to pour His Scriptures into me. I welcome the holy, living Word into my life, and take it deep into my spirit.

Living Lord, may your Word be an incorruptible and ever-living seed in my life. May it take root, and accomplish every good purpose of God through me.

I know that God's Word carries with it the divine power and strength for its own fulfilment. I put my trust in the Word, and in God's Word alone.

I confess again that the Bible is God's living Word, and I hold to its truth at all times and in every situation.

May my words and my heart be acceptable in Your sight, O Lord, my Strength and my Redeemer."

11

Blessing

God is eternal and God is infinite; and this means that every part of His nature is without any limitation. His love, His goodness, His grace, His power, His mercy, all endure forever.

Psalm 136 underlines this by rejoicing *twenty-six times* that 'the steadfast love of the Lord endures forever'.

God so overflows with gracious goodness that He loves to pour it on others. He wants to bless you so that, like Him, you can bless those around you.

When God called Abram, He promised to bless him *and* to make Abram a blessing. As you open your life to the blessing of God, you will be filled to overflowing! God's goodness in-and-upon you will become so obvious that others will want to enjoy Him too! Hallelujah!

Many people look at God through the eyes of religion rather than the eyes of faith. Religion sees God as harsh, unyielding and angry - as one who places impossible burdens upon people.

Nothing could be further from the truth, my friend. It is *human-made religion* which binds heavy burdens upon people's backs. The Father is not like that!

He stands for abundant joy and blessing; for health and wholeness; for light, love, life and truth. This is a far cry from the religious view of God!

The Bible declares that, in Christ, we have been blessed with every spiritual blessing in heavenly places. This shows *where* the blessings are found and *how* they come to us.

It's true that you stood under the judgement of God when you were a sinner. But, on the cross, Jesus secured all God's blessings for you, and removed God's wrath for ever! Now you are blessed in Christ! Everything He has accomplished is available to you - as you believe.

The blessings of God are found only in Jesus, but they are brought to you by the Spirit, and they are activated in you by the Spirit.

Some leaders say that God blessed His people physically in the Old Testament; but that He offers only spiritual blessings in the New Testament.

Do they think God has forgotten that we have physical needs? Remember, dear friend, Jesus assured us that our heavenly Father knows we need such things. That's why He's made every blessing available in Christ, through the Spirit.

The blessing of Abraham is yours

When Jesus died, He carried the curse of the Law. This fulfilled the Scripture which states, 'Cursed is everyone who hangs on a tree'.

But the curse He carried was not His own. It was ours. The Jews were under the curse of the Law, and Jesus carried it on the cross. He also bore the curse on the Gentiles, so that whoever believes in Him could receive the blessing of Abraham.

This great blessing begins with *justification*, with being declared righteous by faith. And it leads on to the quintessence of blessing, to the Holy Spirit - and to *everything* that He imparts into our lives.

The Bible is crammed full of promises for blessing, and God wants you to benefit from every one of them! Believe God now, my friend, for the precise blessing that you need from Him today!

God's words for you

I will bless you and make your name great; and you shall be a blessing. I will bless those who bless you, and I will curse him who curses you. *Genesis 12:2-3*

O Lord, You are the portion of my inheritance and my cup; You maintain my lot. The lines have fallen to me in pleasant places; yes, I have a good inheritance. *Psalm 16:5-6*

You will show me the path of life; in Your presence is fullness of joy; at Your right hand are pleasures for evermore. *Psalm 16:11*

Blessed be the God and Father of our Lord Jesus Christ, who has blessed us with every spiritual blessing in the heavenly places in Christ. *Ephesians 1:3*

Christ has redeemed us from the curse of the law, having become a curse for us… that the blessing of Abraham might come upon the Gentiles in Christ Jesus, that we might receive the promise of the Spirit through faith. *Galatians 3:13-14*

Bless the Lord, O my soul; and all that is within me, bless His holy name! Bless the Lord, O my soul, and forget not all His benefits. *Psalm 103:1-2*

Not returning evil for evil or reviling for reviling, but on the contrary blessing, knowing that you were called to this, that you may inherit a blessing. *1 Peter 3:9*

The blessing of the Lord makes one rich, and He adds no sorrow with it. *Proverbs 10:22*

A faithful man will abound with blessings, but he who hastens to be rich will not go unpunished. *Proverbs 28:20*

How shall I curse whom God has not cursed? And how shall I denounce whom the Lord has not denounced? *Numbers 23:8*

God is not a man, that He should lie, nor a son of man, that He should repent. Has He said, and will He not do? Or has He spoken, and will He not make it good? Behold, I have received a command to bless; He has blessed, and I cannot reverse it. *Numbers 23:19-20*

The Lord bless you and keep you; the Lord make His face shine upon you, and be gracious to you; the Lord lift up His countenance upon you, and give you peace. *Numbers 6:24-26*

So you shall serve the Lord your God, and He will bless your bread and your water. And I will take sickness away from the midst of you. *Exodus 23:25*

May the Lord God of your fathers make you a thousand times more numerous than you are, and bless you as He has promised you! *Deuteronomy 1:11*

He will love you and bless you and multiply you…You shall be blessed above all peoples… And the Lord will take away from you all sickness. *Deuteronomy 7:13-15*

thanks in everything

...e people wonder how it can be possible to ...nk God in *all* circumstances. Surely God ...esn't expect us to thank Him when things go ...rong? He does, my friend, He does!

You see, things look very different from God's perspective. He views a much bigger picture than us. What may look grim to us now, will eventually work out to God's glory. His Word guarantees this.

...d's gracious nature - His goodness and ... kindness - remain infinite and constant, ... circumstances.

Your faith declaration

"I bless the Lord, the God who is my hope and salvation. He is the High God of all blessing and honour and praise.

I confess and declare that I am blessed with every blessing in Christ. He withholds no good thing from me. He has called me to inherit His goodness; and His mercy is always upon me.

I have been released from the curse of the Law, and have been given the blessing of Abraham. Jesus Himself became my curse so that I could receive the blessing of His Spirit.

I now set the direction of my life towards the blessing of God. I apply the blood of Jesus to every curse made against me, and I cancel every negative word spoken about me.

I know that the devil cannot curse those whom God has blessed. The peace of God is within me; the joy of the Lord is my strength; and I receive His divine benefits every day.

My life is now a blessing to others. I give to them whatever God gives to me. I am the Lord's chosen possession, and He is my portion forever."

12

Thanksgiving

In the last few chapters, I've been reminding you about some of the marvellous promises of God which He's given you in the Bible. I trust that you've been receiving these blessings and declaring them in faith and confidence.

Now it is time for us to pause for a special time of *thanksgiving to the Lord!*

Thanksgiving is closely related to praise, and yet the two are different. Thanksgiving is directed completely towards God, whereas praise is mainly acknowledging God before other people. We'll consider praise in chapter eighteen.

Whenever you thank
deep appreciation for what
Remember that you are called
is why thanks*giving* is often calle

It's good to mix spoken thanks wit
act of giving to God. When you give
and show Him your gratitude, you com
blessing. You return thanks to the One from
all blessings flow. How much thanks do you t
He deserves? And how much do you give Him

Give

Som
tha
do
w

Three functions of thanksgiving

Thanksgiving is part

12

Thanksgiving

In the last few chapters, I've been reminding you about some of the marvellous promises of God which He's given you in the Bible. I trust that you've been receiving these blessings and declaring them in faith and confidence.

Now it is time for us to pause for a special time of *thanksgiving to the Lord!*

Thanksgiving is closely related to praise, and yet the two are different. Thanksgiving is directed completely towards God, whereas praise is mainly acknowledging God before other people. We'll consider praise in chapter eighteen.

Your faith declaration

"I bless the Lord, the God who is my hope and salvation. He is the High God of all blessing and honour and praise.

I confess and declare that I am blessed with every blessing in Christ. He withholds no good thing from me. He has called me to inherit His goodness; and His mercy is always upon me.

I have been released from the curse of the Law, and have been given the blessing of Abraham. Jesus Himself became my curse so that I could receive the blessing of His Spirit.

I now set the direction of my life towards the blessing of God. I apply the blood of Jesus to every curse made against me, and I cancel every negative word spoken about me.

I know that the devil cannot curse those whom God has blessed. The peace of God is within me; the joy of the Lord is my strength; and I receive His divine benefits every day.

My life is now a blessing to others. I give to them whatever God gives to me. I am the Lord's chosen possession, and He is my portion forever."

It is good to give thanks to the Lord, and to sing praises to Your name, O Most High; To declare Your loving kindness in the morning, and Your faithfulness every night.

Psalm 92:1-2

Enter into His gates with thanksgiving, and into His courts with praise. Be thankful to Him, and bless His name. For the Lord is good; His mercy is everlasting, and His truth endures to all generations. *Psalm 100:4-5*

Oh, give thanks to the Lord, for He is good! For His mercy endures forever.

Oh, give thanks to the God of gods! For His mercy endures forever.

Oh, give thanks to the Lord of lords! For His mercy endures forever. *Psalm 136:1-3*

Stand every morning to thank and praise the Lord, and likewise at evening. *1 Chronicles 23:30*

Let them sacrifice the sacrifices of thanksgiving, and declare His works with rejoicing. *Psalm 107:22*

Whatever you do in word or deed, do all in the name of the Lord Jesus, giving thanks to God the Father through Him. *Colossians 3:17*

Amen! Blessing and glory and wisdom, thanksgiving and honour and power and might, be to our God forever and ever. Amen. *Revelation 7:12*

God be thanked that though you were slaves of sin, yet you obeyed from the heart that form of doctrine to which you were delivered. *Romans 6:17*

Giving thanks always for all things to God the Father in the name of our Lord Jesus Christ. *Ephesians 5:20*

Thanks be to God for His indescribable gift! *2 Corinthians 9:15*

All things are for your sakes, that grace, having spread through the many, may cause thanksgiving to abound to the glory of God. *2 Corinthians 4:15*

Thanks be to God, who gives us the victory through our Lord Jesus Christ. *1 Corinthians 15:57*

Therefore I exhort first of all that supplications, prayers, intercessions, and giving of thanks be made for all men. *1 Timothy 2:1*

While you are enriched in everything for all liberality, which causes thanksgiving through us to God. For the administration of this service not only supplies the needs of the saints, but also is abounding through many thanksgivings to God. *2 Corinthians 9:11-12*

As you have received Christ Jesus the Lord, so walk in Him, rooted and built up in Him and established in the faith, as you have been taught, abounding in it with thanksgiving. *Colossians 2:6-7*

Now therefore, our God, we thank You and praise Your glorious name. *1 Chronicles 29:13*

Whatever you do in word or deed, do all in the name of the Lord Jesus, giving thanks to God the Father through Him. *Colossians 3:17*

Your faith declaration

"Lord God, Creator of heaven and earth, my Redeemer and Father, I come before You with grateful thanksgiving. I thank You for Your goodness, Your mercy, Your grace and Your truth.

I bless Your Name for Your loving kindness to me each morning, and for Your faithfulness to me every night.

I thank You for Your presence with me at all times. I thank You for never leaving me or forsaking me. I thank You for providing so generously, and for taking care of me in all my circumstances.

I rejoice in Your Son's triumphant victory at the cross. And I thank You for resurrecting Him from the dead, for giving Him all things, and for sending Your Holy Spirit upon me.

I wonder at Your love and patience, and I thank You for remembering my sins and iniquities no more.

Thank You, Father, that Jesus is coming again soon, and that then I will be with You forever in Your heavenly kingdom. Amen."

13

Healing

Jesus is the same, yesterday, today and for ever! He's still doing today everything that He did when He walked on this earth. He hasn't changed a bit!

Jesus is seated at the right hand of the Father, at the highest place of the universe, and He is your Healer. Nothing is beyond His power or control. And He longs to release you from all sickness.

Some people don't believe that Jesus has ever healed anyone. Others think that healing miracles were only for biblical times. Many believers have been taught that sickness is God's will for their lives. My friend, these common attitudes rob God's people of Christ's healing power.

It's a basic biblical fact that God is a healing God. He introduced Himself to the people of Israel with these words, *'I am the Lord who heals you.'* This is a central covenant promise, and was God's first promise after Israel had left Egypt.

After Jesus had survived His encounter with the enemy in the desert, He also introduced Himself to Israel as the One who was *'sent to heal'*.

This shows us that healing is central to God's nature, and at the heart of His dealings with His people. It's why Jesus ministered to the sick, and it's why He wants to make you whole.

Sickness is part of Satan's rebel kingdom, and it points to sin - which lies at the root of all sickness. This is why Jesus hates sickness so much.

Sickness didn't exist until sin came into the world. This doesn't mean that your sickness must be the result of your personal sin. It's more likely that your sickness is a consequence of the general sinful, polluted condition of the whole world.

He forgives sins and heals sickness

When Jesus served on earth, He forgave sinners *and* healed the sick. His power to heal revealed His authority to forgive. The one pointed to the other.

Jesus has exactly the same authority today to heal all your sickness and to forgive your every sin.

He carried your sickness on the cross, and struck at the root of sickness, at sin. Once sin had been dealt with, God's healing could properly begin. This is the good news of the gospel of Jesus Christ.

But, dear friend, Jesus' healing ministry is a sign which points towards something far more glorious than even the best healing on earth.

All healing is just a tiny foretaste of the future glory of God, which will be dramatically revealed at the resurrection, at the total transformation of the body. When that day comes, my friend, you won't need healing again - for you'll never get sick again!

This hope is a real comfort for people who do not experience healing on earth. Keep on believing God for your healing. Never give up through discouragement or doubt. Remember, Jesus never fails. He was, He is, and He will be your Healer.

My friend, take all these promises of God for healing and let the Holy Spirit touch you today at your point of need.

But, as you do this, please remember that your real hope is for the future kingdom when you'll experience *every* blessing to the *full*.

God's words for you

If you heed the voice of the Lord your God, and do wha is right in His sight, give ear to His commandments and keep all His statutes, I will put none of the diseases on you which I have brought on the Egyptians. For I am the Lord who heals you. *Exodus 15:2*

Who forgives all your iniquities, who heals all your diseases. *Psalm 103:*

Surely He has borne our grief and carried our sorrows. H was wounded for our transgressions, He was bruised for our iniquities; the chastisement for our peace was upon Him, and by His stripes we are healed. *Isaiah 53:4-*

He sent His word and healed them, and delivered them from their destruction. *Psalm 107:2*

Which is easier, to say, 'Your sins are forgiven you,' or to say, 'Arise, take up your bed and walk'? That you may know the Son of Man has power on earth to forgive sins, He said to the paralytic, 'I say to you, arise, take up your bed, and go your way to your house.' *Mark 2:9-1*

God anointed Jesus of Nazareth with the Holy Spirit and with power, who went about doing good and healing all who were oppressed by the devil, for God was with Him. *Acts 10:3*

They brought to Him many who were demon-possessed. And He cast out the spirits with a word, and healed all who were sick, that it might be fulfilled which was spoke by Isaiah the prophet, saying: 'He Himself took our infirmities and bore our sicknesses.' *Matthew 8:16-*

Who Himself bore our sins in His own body on the tree, that we, having died to sins, might live for righteousness by whose stripes you were healed. *1 Peter 2:24*

My son, give attention to My words; incline your ear to My sayings. Do not let them depart from your eyes; keep them in the midst of your heart; For they are life to those who find them, and health to all their flesh.

Proverbs 4:20-22

And Jesus, moved with compassion, put out His hand and touched him, and said to him, 'I am willing; be cleansed.'

Mark 1:41

Jesus said to him, 'If you can believe, all things are possible to him who believes.' *Mark 9:23*

He also brought them out with silver and gold, and there was none feeble among His tribes. *Psalm 105:37*

Great multitudes followed Him, and He healed them all.

Matthew 12:15

Beloved, I pray that you may prosper in all things and be in health, just as your soul prospers. *3 John 1:2*

So ought not this woman, being a daughter of Abraham, whom Satan has bound - think of it - for eighteen years, be loosed from this bond on the Sabbath? *Luke 13:16*

Jesus answered and said to her, 'O woman, great is your faith! Let it be to you as you desire.' And her daughter was healed from that very hour. *Matthew 15:26-28*

He touched their eyes, saying, 'According to your faith let it be to you.' *Matthew 9:29*

Your faith declaration

"I confess and declare that God is the Great Healer. He has established a binding healing covenant with me through the blood of His Son Christ Jesus.

I know that it's God's nature to heal, and it's His will to heal me and make me whole. He sends His healing Word; and His Holy Spirit carries a healing anointing into my body, my soul and my spirit.

Jesus Himself took my infirmities, bore my sicknesses, and healed me by His stripes. I know that all those who touch Him are made completely whole, and I press in by faith to touch Jesus now.

I choose not to be moved by what I see or feel with my natural senses. I trust God's goodness and power to heal me.

I choose life, not death. I reject sickness and disease as the devil's work. God's loving kindness and tender-hearted compassion surround me.

I walk with Jesus as my Healer, and I commit myself into the hands of the Great Physician. I am listening to His healing words and following His path for my healing."

14

Abundance

My dear friend, I hope you know that Jesus came to bring you the full-and-abundant life of His wonderful heavenly kingdom.

He didn't come to make you miserable or depressed. He came to lead you into His kingdom of light and life, and to encourage you to seek His rule, His kingdom, before everything else.

This kingdom life is the rich and lavish spiritual life of God Himself, which overflows from Him into His creation. When God made the world, He provided for it from within Himself – in extravagant abundance. It was teeming with perfect life!

When Jesus came on the Father's rescue mission to our ruined planet, He came in the fullness of His abundant divine life to establish God's holy rule in our fallen human lives.

I'm sure you know this means that we must submit to the personal rule of the Father through Jesus the Son. We do this through the Holy Spirit, who is the extravagant life of the kingdom.

Although living in God's kingdom means discipline, obedience, service and mission; the kingdom life is not always meant to be a spartan, ascetic existence. Within the kingdom, there's abundant provision for every part of our lives.

This is why Jesus tells you not to worry about the daily necessities of life. In the Bible, He's shown you that there's no need to worry about what you eat, or drink, or wear. This is because your loving heavenly Father already knows what you need.

Jesus has instructed you to make God's kingdom the first priority in your life. And He's promised that, when you do this, all your needs will be met.

Do you know what Jesus means by this? He's saying that your Father will provide you with *everything in abundance* - as you trust Him and put Him first in your life. Isn't that a glorious promise?

The extravagant abundance of the kingdom touches every area of your life.

⇒ You can enjoy His blessing in your spirit.

⇒ You can enjoy it in your emotional life, as you overflow with joy, peace and well being.

⇒ And you can know His provision materially, so that your physical needs are properly met.

Of course, just as God's abundance overflows from Him to you, so He expects His extravagant provision to overflow from you to others.

He keeps on providing for you spiritually because He loves you personally. But He longs for you to pass your spiritual life on to others in need.

He goes on providing for you emotionally because He's dedicated to your wholeness. But He wants you to respond to His grace by serving hurting people in a similar therapeutic way.

And He continually provides for you materially because He's the ultimate Giver. But He aches for you to give to the poor in His extravagant fashion.

My friend, take hold of God's abundant life today! Seek His kingdom first! And then start sharing it extravagantly with others!

God's words for you

Let the wicked forsake his way, and the unrighteous man his thoughts; let him return to the Lord, and He will have mercy on him; and to our God, for He will abundantly pardon. *Isaiah 55:7*

The thief does not come except to steal, and to kill, and to destroy. I have come that they may have life, and that they may have it more abundantly. *John 10:10*

I say to you that even Solomon in all his glory was not arrayed like one of these. *Matthew 6:29*

Do not worry about tomorrow, for tomorrow will worry about its own things. Sufficient for the day is its own trouble. *Matthew 6:34*

Beloved, I pray that you may prosper in all things and be in health, just as your soul prospers. *3 John 1:2*

Seek first the kingdom of God and His righteousness, and all these things shall be added to you. *Matthew 6:33*

You cannot serve God and mammon. *Matthew 6:24*

Give, and it will be given to you: good measure, pressed down, shaken together, and running over will be put into your bosom. For with the same measure that you use, it will be measured back to you. *Luke 6:38*

Both riches and honour come from You, and You reign over all. In Your hand is power and might; in Your hand it is to make great and to give strength to all.
1 Chronicles 29:12

There is one who scatters, yet increases more; and there is one who withholds more than is right, but it leads to poverty. *Proverbs 11:24*

The generous soul will be made rich, and he who waters will also be watered himself. *Proverbs 11:25*

God, who is rich in mercy, because of His great love with which He loved us. *Ephesians 2:4*

Command those who are rich in this present age not to be haughty, nor to trust in uncertain riches but in the living God, who gives us richly all things to enjoy. *1 Timothy 6:17*

My God shall supply all your needs according to His riches in glory by Christ Jesus. *Philippians 4:19*

This I say: He who sows sparingly will also reap sparingly, and he who sows bountifully will also reap bountifully. *2 Corinthians 9:6*

God is able to make all grace abound toward you, that you, always having all sufficiency in all things, may have an abundance for every good work. *2 Corinthians 9:8*

Do not love sleep, lest you come to poverty; open your eyes, and you will be satisfied with bread. *Proverbs 20:13*

A little sleep, a little slumber, a little folding of the hands to sleep - so shall your poverty come on you like a prowler, and your need like an armed man. *Proverbs 6:10-11*

Do not fear, little flock, for it is your Father's good pleasure to give you the kingdom. *Luke 12:33*

Your faith declaration

"I confess and declare that the All-Creating, All-Providing God is my infinite source and supply. Because He is my Father, my shepherd, my vine, my bread and my cup, I have all that I ever need.

I am seeking my Father's kingdom before everything else in this life, and I am living as a child of His care.

I set my heart towards God, and trust Him for His bountiful supply. I am becoming a giver like God, and am blessed in all my giving.

I am a generous sower of good seed, and I am set for an abundant harvest. I am diligent and persistent in doing good at all times.

I know that I will prosper in all things and be in health, just as my soul prospers.

The Father who wills abundance for His children is giving me all things richly to enjoy.

I praise God for His extravagant provision, for His lavish answers to my deepest needs, for His enduring steadfast love. And I am watching now for His abundance in every part of my life."

15

Power

Our God is the all-powerful Being who is before and beyond, above and below, in and throughout our entire universe.

Because He's both infinite and eternal, there can be no other god, and there can be no end to His absolute power. Quite simply, He is All Mighty.

This evening, my friend, stand outside your home and gaze at the stars. See what He's made by the greatness of His power. Realise that He knows all by name. And worship your all-powerful Maker.

This mighty Being is also the Sustainer of all things. As the stars move round the heavenlies, and as our world spins and moves through the seasons, He holds everything together. He upholds all life. He is *your* Sustainer - He is the One who gives *you* His strength for your *every* weakness.

The almighty, all-powerful Maker of heaven and earth is your personal Enabler. Alongside every command for you, and every call of God to you, His divine enabling comes for you to fulfil it.

The Father wills and initiates His good and perfect plan for your life. The Son of God, through His work on the cross, has accomplished God's plan. And the Spirit now comes to enable you to find and fulfil God's purposes for your life.

It is God Himself who is working in you, enabling you to fulfil His will. Remember, you cannot do this without the Holy Spirit. God's call upon your life can never be fulfilled in your own strength. The Lord of Hosts has spoken: you cannot live by might or by power, only by His Spirit.

God's creative and sustaining power is freely available through the Holy Spirit, who is the gift of the ascended Christ to His people. And Jesus has promised that God's own Holy Spirit will clothe you with His almighty power.

Wherever you go, you have this divine power upon you. The Spirit is present in-and-with you, moving you in the direction of God's will.

This means that you can find holy strength at your times of greatest weakness. God calls you to exchange your weakness for His strength, and to begin to do the impossible with Him.

So be bold! Be strong! Be confident in the God who has called you! He's utterly reliable, and He will enable you to do whatever He calls you to do.

God's words for you

He gives power to the weak, and to those who have no might He increases strength. *Isaiah 40:29*

Those who wait on the Lord shall renew their strength; they shall mount up with wings like eagles, they shall run and not be weary, they shall walk and not faint. *Isaiah 40:31*

The Lord has established His throne in heaven, and His kingdom rules over all. *Psalm 103:19*

Yours is the kingdom and the power and the glory for ever. Amen. *Matthew 6:13*

We give You thanks, O Lord God Almighty, the One who is and who was and who is to come, because You have taken Your great power and reigned. *Revelation 11:17*

Whatever the Lord pleases He does, in heaven and in earth, in the seas and in all deep places. *Psalm 135:6*

And I heard, as it were, the voice of a great multitude, as the sound of many waters and as the sound of mighty thunderings, saying, "Alleluia! For the Lord God Omnipotent reigns! *Revelation 19:6*

With men this is impossible, but with God all things are possible. *Matthew 19:26*

I can do all things through Christ who strengthens me. *Philippians 4:13*

Is anything too hard for the Lord? *Genesis 18:14*

The eyes of your understanding being enlightened; that you may know what is the exceeding greatness of His power toward us who believe, according to the working of His mighty power. *Ephesians 1:18-19*

Christ, the power of God and the wisdom of God. *1 Corinthians 1:24*

I am not ashamed of the gospel of Christ, for it is the power of God to salvation for everyone who believes, for the Jew first and also for the Greek. *Romans 1:16*

Behold, I send the Promise of My Father upon you; but tarry in the city of Jerusalem until you are endued with power from on high. *Luke 24:49*

You shall receive power when the Holy Spirit has come upon you; and you shall be witnesses to Me in Jerusalem, and in all Judea and Samaria, and to the end of the earth. *Acts 1:8*

His divine power has given to us all things that pertain to life and godliness, through the knowledge of Him who called us by glory and virtue. *2 Peter 1:3*

'Not by might nor by power, but by My Spirit,' says the Lord of hosts. *Zechariah 4:6*

God has not given us a spirit of fear, but of power and of love and of a sound mind. *2 Timothy 1:7*

For the message of the cross is foolishness to those who are perishing, but to us who are being saved it is the power of God. *1 Corinthians 1:18*

I became a minister according to the gift of the grace of God given to me by the effective working of His power. *Ephesians 3:7*

Now to Him who is able to do exceedingly abundantly above all that we ask or think, according to the power that works in us. *Ephesians 3:20*

Work out your own salvation with fear and trembling, for it is God who works in you both to will and to do for His good pleasure. *Philippians 2:12-13*

Though He was crucified in weakness, yet He lives by the power of God. For we also are weak in Him, but we shall live with Him by the power of God. *2 Corinthians 13:4*

My grace is sufficient for you, for My strength is made perfect in weakness. Therefore most gladly I will rather boast in my infirmities, that the power of Christ may rest upon me. For when I am weak, then I am strong. *2 Corinthians 12:9-10*

Your faith declaration

"I confess and declare that I can do nothing without Christ. I have nothing, am nothing and will always be nothing without Him.

Yet I know that everything is possible with Him, and that I can do all things through Christ who strengthens me. He gives courage to my faint heart. His strength is made perfect in my weakness. Nothing is impossible for me by faith in His power.

God's power is absolute, and His kingdom rules over all. His throne is eternal, and He laughs at His enemies. Nothing is too difficult for the One who holds the universe in the palm of His hand, who views the nations as drops in the ocean.

I cease from my strivings and worry, and trust all my circumstances to God. He works all things for His glory, and for the good of those who love Him.

I thank the Father for His exceedingly great and super-abundant power which is at work within me. He is enabling me to do all His good pleasure.

I am not trusting in my own might or power, but in the Spirit of the Lord. I know that my Father's grace is all that I need."

16

Victory

Jesus is the Winner of winners! He's the Champion of the World! He's the totally triumphant Victor! He's the all-prevailing, ever-conquering first-and-foremost God. And He has presented *you* with His victory, with His world championship!

That's right, my friend! Christ's victory is *yours*, in Jesus' name – it's a free-and-unconditional gift!

It's time you realised that Jesus really is victorious over all the power of the enemy!

⇒ He overcame the tempter in the wilderness.

⇒ He pushed back the devil in His ministry of miracles.

⇒ He resisted the adversary in the garden of Gethsemane.

⇒ He smashed the destroyer on the cross.

⇒ And He rose triumphant over Satan in His mighty resurrection.

One day, Jesus is coming back to the earth to demonstrate His victory to the whole world. And, when He does, *you will share in that triumph.*

As a believer, you've already overcome the evil one through the victory of your faith. The anointing that you have received from God has broken the heavy yoke of bondage in your life.

And, through the name of Jesus, you have God's own authority to tread upon serpents and scorpions. My friend, you share Christ's power over all the force of the enemy!

You're the world champion

God wants you to use the victory that He's given you. He wants you to live in His victory as a world-champion, super-heavyweight overcomer!

It's time for you to stop running away from the devil. Turn round and face Him, in Jesus' name. Resist him now, and he will run away from you!

The Lord of Hosts has transformed you into a far better warrior than Samson. You're a conqueror fit to take on the Goliaths of our day. You're an Elijah who can face down the false prophets of today.

Enter into His victory now! Start flexing your spiritual muscles! Use these promises to enforce His victory over every rebellious circumstance in-and-around your life.

God's words for you

I am He who lives, and was dead, and behold, I am alive for evermore. Amen. And I have the keys of Hades and of Death. *Revelation 1:18*

He raised Him from the dead and seated Him at His right hand in the heavenly places, far above all principality and power and might and dominion, and every name that is named, not only in this age but also in that which is to come. *Ephesians 1:20-21*

Thanks be to God, who gives us the victory through our Lord Jesus Christ. *1 Corinthians 15:57*

He must reign till He has put all enemies under His feet. *1 Corinthians 15:25*

He put all things under His feet, and gave Him to be head over all things to the church. *Ephesians 1:22*

We are more than conquerors through Him who loved us. *Romans 8:37*

The last enemy that will be destroyed is death.
1 Corinthians 15:25-26

The horse is prepared for the day of battle, but deliverance is of the Lord. *Proverbs 21:31*

The Lord does not save with sword and spear; for the battle is the Lord's. *1 Samuel 17:47*

Lift up your heads, O you gates! And be lifted up, you everlasting doors! And the King of glory shall come in. Who is this King of glory? The Lord strong and mighty, the Lord mighty in battle. *Psalm 24:7-8*

Do not be afraid. Stand still, and see the salvation of the Lord, which He will accomplish for you today. The Lord will fight for you. *Exodus 14:13-14*

I will sing to the Lord, for He has triumphed gloriously! The horse and its rider he has thrown into the sea!
Exodus 15:1

You have armed me with strength for the battle; You have subdued under me those who rose up against me.
Psalm 18:39-40

Behold, I give you the authority to trample on serpents and scorpions, and over all the power of the enemy, and nothing shall by any means hurt you. *Luke 10:19*

By You I can run against a troop, by my God I can leap over a wall. *Psalm 18:29*

I have written to you, young men, because you are strong, and the Word of God abides in you, and you have overcome the wicked one. *1 John 2:14*

I have pursued my enemies and overtaken them; neither did I turn back again till they were destroyed. *Psalm 18:37*

The weapons of our warfare are not carnal but mighty in God for pulling down strongholds, casting down arguments and every high thing that exalts itself against the knowledge of God, bringing every thought into captivity to the obedience of Christ. *2 Corinthians 10:4-5*

He teaches my hands to make war, so that my arms can bend a bow of bronze. *Psalm 18:34*

Whatever is born of God overcomes the world. And this is the victory that has overcome the world - our faith. *1 John 5:4*

It is God who arms me with strength, and makes my way perfect. *Psalm 18:32*

Be strong in the Lord and in the power of His might. *Ephesians 6:10*

Therefore take up the whole armour of God, that you may be able to withstand in the evil day, and having done all, to stand. *Ephesians 6:13*

Therefore submit to God. Resist the devil and he will flee from you. *James 4:7*

To him who overcomes I will grant to sit with Me on My throne, as I also overcame and sat down with My Father on His throne. *Revelation 3:21*

The God of peace will crush Satan under your feet shortly. *Romans 16:20*

Your faith declaration

"I confess and declare that Jesus Christ is the Champion of champions. He is the totally triumphant Victor, the all-prevailing, ever-conquering King of kings and Lord of lords.

I rejoice that the devil has been defeated, disarmed, destroyed and driven out. In the mighty name of Jesus, I have full authority over Satan and all his evil works in my life. Even demons are subject to me in Jesus' name!

But I rejoice even more that I am being saved, sanctified and strengthened by Christ. He has given me His victory and made me more than a conqueror. I am clothed with the garments of holiness and am equipped with the armour of God.

I am standing against the evil one. I am resisting his works. I set myself on the path of freedom and utterly reject every evil power. God is training my hands for war and He does battle for me.

I will sing to the Lord for He has triumphed gloriously. The Lord who is strong and mighty is my strength and my song. He has become my salvation. Praise His holy name."

17

Protection

Throughout the Scriptures, especially in the Old Testament, God is revealed as 'the Most High', as the great protector of His people.

My dear friend, the Bible proclaims that God is your refuge and strength. He's your encircling shield and mighty stronghold. He's your shelter and support, your citadel and saving fortress, your sanctuary and strong tower, your battlement and rock. The Most High God is Himself your saviour, your deliverer and your protector.

Do not doubt God's power and willingness to protect you. His arms always uphold you. He sends His angels to protect you and to keep you safe. He has rescued you from the snare of the fowler. And He will *continue* to deliver you from all harm.

⇒ There's total security in *the name of Jesus*! His name is your place of safety. Always call upon the name of Jesus for your protection.

⇒ There's absolute safety in *the blood of Jesus*! His precious blood brings you freedom and security in God. The devil cannot stand before the blood.

⇒ And there's full protection in *the armour of God*, which He's given you. This provides you with head-to-toe protection when you're wrestling with the spiritual forces of the enemy.

A life-style which protects

The armour of God is a life-style that you must live. Each item represents God's varied provision for your daily walk with Him - truth, peace, faith, righteousness, hope and the Word of God.

The sword of the Spirit is a particularly powerful weapon against the enemy. It's the special Word of God, given to you by the Holy Spirit, to help you win your battles. Draw it from your belt of truth, dear friend, and use it against the devil in your life.

Learn to recognise and use the special, 'now' words of the Spirit. Like Jesus, you can defend yourself against every onslaught of the enemy with the powerful words, 'It is written!'

Have total confidence in God's protection! Let Him drive away every fear of the enemy! Make your declaration of faith today and every day.

God's words for you

The Lord also will be a refuge for the oppressed, a refuge in times of trouble. *Psalm 9:9*

He that dwells in the secret place of the Most High shall abide under the shadow of the Almighty. I will say of the Lord, 'He is my refuge and my fortress; my God, in Him I will trust.' *Psalm 91:1-2*

He shall cover you with His feathers, and under His wings you shall take refuge; his truth shall be your shield and buckler. *Psalm 91:4*

Because you have made the Lord, who is my refuge, even the Most High, your dwelling place, no evil shall befall you, nor shall any plague come near your dwelling. *Psalm 91:9-10*

He shall give His angels charge over you, to keep you in all your ways. *Psalm 91:11*

May the Lord answer you in the day of trouble; may the name of the God of Jacob defend you. *Psalm 20:1*

I know that the Lord saves His anointed; He will answer him from His holy heaven with the saving strength of His right hand. *Psalm 20:6*

Some trust in chariots, and some in horses; but we will remember the name of the Lord our God. *Psalm 20:6*

He shall deliver you in six troubles, yes, in seven no evil shall touch you. *Job 5:19*

The Lord will deliver me from every evil work and preserve me for His heavenly kingdom. *2 Timothy 4:18*

You shall be hidden from the scourge of the tongue, and you shall not be afraid of destruction when it comes. *Job 5:20*

The eternal God is your refuge, and underneath are the everlasting arms; He will thrust out the enemy from before you, and will say, 'Destroy!' *Deuteronomy 33:27*

God is our refuge and strength, a very present help in trouble. *Psalm 46:1*

The Lord has been my defence, and my God the rock of my refuge. *Psalm 94:22*

From the end of the earth I will cry to You, when my heart is overwhelmed; lead me to the rock that is higher than I. For You have been a shelter for me, a strong tower from the enemy. I will abide in Your tabernacle forever; I will trust in the shelter of Your wings. *Psalm 61:2-4*

I give you the authority to trample on serpents and scorpions, and over all the power of the enemy, and nothing shall by any means hurt you. *Luke 10:19*

The Lord is my rock and my fortress and my deliverer.
2 Samuel 22:1

The name of the Lord is a strong tower; the righteous run to it and are safe. *Proverbs 18:10*

The God of my strength, in whom I will trust; my shield and the horn of my salvation, my stronghold and my refuge; my Saviour, You save me from violence.
2 Samuel 22:2

These signs will follow those who believe: In My name they will cast out demons; they will speak with new tongues; they will take up serpents; and if they drink anything deadly, it will by no means hurt them.
Mark 16:17-18

You are kept by the power of God through faith for salvation ready to be revealed in the last time. *1 Peter 1:5*

I will lift up my eyes to the hills - from whence comes my help? My help comes from the Lord, who made heaven and earth. *Psalm 121:1-8*

The Lord shall preserve you from all evil; He shall preserve your soul. The Lord shall preserve your going out and your coming in from this time forth, and even forevermore. *Psalm 121:7-8*

When you pass through the waters, I will be with you; and through the rivers, they shall not overflow you. When you walk through the fire, you shall not be burned, nor shall the flame scorch you. *Isaiah 43:2*

The Lord is good, a stronghold in the day of trouble; and He knows those who trust in Him. *Nahum 1:7*

Your faith declaration

"I confess and declare that I dwell in the secret place of God Most High, and that I rest under His holy protection. My heavenly Father is watching over me by night and by day.

God is my shelter and my refuge. He is my help, my hope and my comfort. No evil will ever harm me or draw near to my dwelling, for my Father sends His angels to guard me and to keep me safe.

The Lord preserves my going out and my coming in. He is the protector of the faithful, and He saves me from the violence and oppression of the enemy.

I do not fear anything, for the Almighty is the fortress of my life. He is my citadel and support, my bastion and battlement, the rock of my deliverance. The mighty name of Jesus is my strong protecting tower.

The Lord God Most High is Himself my encircling shield and faithful protector. He is my defence against the scourge of tongues and my saviour from pestilence and destruction. Hallelujah!

The Lord will deliver me from every evil work and preserve me for His heavenly kingdom."

18

Praise

Back in chapter twelve, I showed you that praise is related to thanks. They always go together. You're called to thank God *and* to praise Him in all things.

When you praise God, you extol His virtues to the world. You proclaim His marvellous works. You tell other people about the wonders of God. You declare His excellent qualities to them. This is why praise is both prophetic and evangelistic.

We can thank God privately, but we properly praise Him *publicly*; for praise is mainly given in the presence of other people. Nevertheless, we proclaim our praise *before* God; and we shake the heavenly principalities and powers with our praise.

ollows on from thanksgiving. The Psalms
enter God's presence with thanksgiving,
and then - once we're there - to praise Him!

God deserves your praise. When you think about the praise given to people, you'll want to praise Him even more. Sport stars, media personalities, business achievers, politicians, royalty, even church leaders - they all receive human praise.

How much more, dear friend, should God receive all your honour, all your glory and all your praise!

Praise is an essential part of your calling as a believer. The New Testament states that you've been called from darkness into God's marvellous light - to declare His praises.

And the Psalms teach that God has instructed His children to praise Him - to silence the enemy and the avenger. Praise is a sure-fire way of dealing with your enemy! It's a terrible noise in his ears!

The Bible shows that praise brings victory and deliverance. Even more importantly, it shows that praise brings God - for He inhabits the praise of His people. Isn't that a wonderful reason for praise!

Praise introduces God to the hurting people who need to know Him. It also glorifies God and prepares the way for His blessing to enter your life.

This is why you should learn to praise God at all time. Let His praise be continually in your mouth!

God's words for you

I will bless the LORD at all times; His praise shall continually be in my mouth. *Psalm 34:1*

Praise the Lord! Praise God in His sanctuary; praise Him in His mighty firmament!
Praise Him for His mighty acts; praise Him according to His excellent greatness!
Praise Him with the sound of the trumpet; praise Him with the lute and harp!
Praise Him with the timbrel and dance; praise Him with stringed instruments and flutes!
Praise Him with loud cymbals; praise Him with clashing cymbals!
Let everything that has breath praise the Lord. Praise the Lord! *Psalm 150:1-6*

Let us continually offer the sacrifice of praise to God, that is, the fruit of our lips, giving thanks to His name. *Hebrews 13:15*

O Lord, our Lord, how excellent is Your name in all the earth, who set Your glory above the heavens!
Out of the mouth of babes and nursing infants you have ordained strength, because of Your enemies, that You may silence the enemy and the avenger. *Psalm 8:1-2*

Blessed are You, Lord God of Israel, our Father, forever and ever. *1 Chronicles 29:10*

I will praise You, O Lord, with my whole heart; I will tell of all Your marvellous works. I will be glad and rejoice in You; I will sing praise to Your name, O Most High.

Psalm 9:1-2

Stand up and bless the Lord your God for ever and ever! Blessed be Your glorious name, which is exalted above all blessing and praise! *Nehemiah 9:5*

Bless the Lord, O my soul; and all that is within me, bless His holy name!
Bless the Lord, O my soul, and forget not all His benefits:
Who forgives all your iniquities, who heals all your diseases,
Who redeems your life from destruction, who crowns you with loving kindness and tender mercies
Who satisfies your mouth with good things, so that your youth is renewed like the eagle's. *Psalm 103:1-5*

Violence shall no longer be heard in your land, neither wasting nor destruction within your borders; but you shall call your walls Salvation, and your gates Praise.

Isaiah 60:18

The Lord is my strength and song, and He has become my salvation; He is my God, and I will praise Him; my father's God, and I will exalt Him. *Exodus 15:2*

Who is like You, O Lord? Who is like You, glorious in holiness, fearful in praises, doing wonders? *Exodus 15:11*

For of Him and through Him and to Him are all things, to whom be glory forever. Amen. *Romans 11:36*

Yours, O Lord, is the greatness, the power and the glory, the victory and the majesty; for all that is in heaven and in earth is Yours; Yours is the kingdom, O Lord, and You are exalted as head over all. *1 Chronicles 29:11*

Now to the King eternal, immortal, invisible, to God who alone is wise, be honour and glory forever and ever. Amen. *1 Timothy 1:17*

You are worthy, O Lord, to receive glory and honour and power; for You created all things, and by Your will they exist and were created. *Revelation 4:11*

Who shall not fear You, O Lord, and glorify Your name? For You alone are holy. For all nations shall come and worship before You, for Your judgements have been manifested. *Revelation 15:4*

Blessing and honour and glory and power be to Him who sits on the throne, and to the Lamb, forever and ever!
Revelation 5:13

Great and marvellous are Your works, Lord God Almighty! Just and true are Your ways, O King of the saints!
Revelation 15:3

Blessed be the God and Father of our Lord Jesus Christ, who has blessed us with every spiritual blessing in the heavenly places in Christ. *Ephesians 1:3*

Blessed be the God and Father of our Lord Jesus Christ, who according to His abundant mercy has begotten us again to a living hope through the resurrection of Jesus Christ from the dead. *1 Peter 1:3*

Your faith declaration

"I will bless the Lord at all times. His praise will continually be in my mouth. I will offer Him the sacrifice of my praise in all my circumstances.

I will extol the virtues of my God and my King to all people and before all heavenly powers. For He has delivered me from the bondage of darkness; He has brought me into His marvellous light.

The Lord is my strength and my song, and He has become my salvation. Praise His excellent name!

Who is like unto You, O Lord, glorious in holiness, fearful in praises, doing wonders? For You alone are gracious and merciful, tender-hearted and loving, slow to anger and abounding in steadfast love.

Yours, O Lord, is the greatness, the power, the glory, the victory and the majesty in all the world.

The name of the Lord is holy, and worthy to be praised by all beings. His name is glorious, and is exalted far above all blessing and praise.

Blessing and glory and power be unto Him for ever and ever! Amen!"

19

My family

Your family relationships are meant to be the most precious ties that you have on earth. They're God's gracious gift to you. No society can succeed without stable and godly families.

God is firmly for families. He wants to see your entire family saved, set free and Spirit-filled. God wants to bless your family with salvation, and with all His abundant blessings.

Most of us are used to expecting God to bless us as individual believers; but God also deals with us in families. His promises do not stop with one or two people in your family, they extend to your entire household.

The Bible contains many promises of 'household' salvation. Moses told the children of Israel to sacrifice a lamb for each *household.* When the lamb's blood was splashed on the door-posts and lintels of their home, the whole household was saved from the destroyer in Egypt.

I'm sure you know that the Passover lamb is a picture of Jesus' saving work on the cross. This should be a tremendous encouragement for you to believe God for your family. God wants every member to believe and be saved!

The family is God's idea

Marriage is the foundation of every godly family. Tragically, very many families are being torn apart today by the pressures of our fallen society - by debt, drugs, alcohol, adultery, impatience and an increasing lack of respect for God's way.

God is near to the broken-hearted, and He longs to bind them up. When we're forsaken, He promises to befriend, to heal and to restore.

You may need to have faith for this to happen in your life. And you may need to help your church become a community of grace and forgiveness where the broken-hearted feel genuinely welcome.

God's purpose in marriage is for men and women to live together in unity, in life-long companionship. Even though marriage is just a temporary arrangement for this life only (it's 'til death us do part') it is special to God and sacred to Him.

God made men and women as joint bearers of His corporate image. He commissioned them to be fruitful and to multiply. And He commanded them to fill the earth and to exercise dominion over it.

This mandate can be fulfilled only through Spirit-filled marriages. True Christian marriages, where Christ is the Head, are essential for God's purposes to be fulfilled in the earth.

Promises for your family

As you begin to claim God's promises for your family, please understand that Jesus' blood has already bought them much blessing. Through your faith, the Father really can help your family. You can see the blessings of His covenant come to them - salvation, healing, peace, deliverance, and so on.

The negative elements which have been passed down your family bloodline have been broken by the blood of Jesus. On the cross, He released you from every hereditary curse and demonic bondage.

You can also claim the blessings of God for your children, as the Bible promises that the fruit of the womb is blessed by faith.

May God give you wisdom from His Word, and grace from His Spirit, to live His life in your family situation and to see your family blessed.

God's words for you

The Father of our Lord Jesus Christ, from whom the whole family in heaven and earth is named.

Ephesians 3:14-15

A man shall leave his father and mother and be joined to his wife, and they shall become one flesh. *Genesis 2:24*

Wives, submit to your own husbands, as to the Lord. For the husband is head of the wife, as also Christ is head of the church; and He is the Saviour of the body.

Ephesians 5:22-23

Husbands, likewise, dwell with them with understanding, giving honour to the wife, as to the weaker vessel, and as being heirs together of the grace of life, that your prayers may not be hindered. *1 Peter 3:7*

When he had brought them into his house, he set food before them; and he rejoiced, having believed in God with all his household. *Acts 16:34*

Marriage is honourable among all, and the bed undefiled; but fornicators and adulterers God will judge.

Hebrews 13:4

Children are a heritage from the Lord, the fruit of the womb is a reward. *Psalm 127:3*

Wives, be submissive to your own husbands, that even if some do not obey the Word, they, without a word, may be won by the conduct of their wives. *1 Peter 3:1*

Husbands, love your wives, just as Christ also loved the church and gave Himself for her. *Ephesians 5:25*

Children, obey your parents in the Lord, for this is right. Honour your father and mother, which is the first commandment with promise: that it may be well with you and you may live long on the earth. *Ephesians 6:1-3*

Whoever does the will of My Father in heaven is My brother and sister and mother. *Matthew 12:50*

God sets the solitary in families. *Psalm 68:6*

He who finds a wife finds a good thing, and obtains favour from the Lord. *Proverbs 18:22*

The unbelieving husband is sanctified by the wife, and the unbelieving wife is sanctified by the husband; otherwise your children would be unclean, but now they are holy. *1 Corinthians 7:14*

There are eunuchs who have made themselves eunuchs for the kingdom of heaven's sake. He, who is able to accept it, let him accept it. *Matthew 19:12*

Everyone who has left houses or brothers or sisters or father or mother or wife or children or lands, for My name's sake, shall receive a hundredfold, and inherit eternal life. *Matthew 19:29*

Your faith declaration

"I confess and declare that the living God is my eternal Father and the true Head of my earthly family. He has given me my family, and it is part of His divine purpose for my life.

I know that He is a Father to the fatherless and a Spouse to the single. He takes the lonely and sets them in families. All families come from Him, and He delights to fill them with His blessing.

In the name of Jesus, I claim the protection of the new covenant over my family; I speak words of hope, salvation and healing to my family; and I bless my family with righteousness, peace and joy.

I honour my family relationships as a child of my parents, as a partner of my spouse, and as a parent of my children. May God bless them all richly!

I uphold the covenant of marriage. I honour my father and mother. I esteem my partner as God's precious gift to me. And I rejoice that children are a wonderful heritage from the Lord.

In Jesus' name, I release my family from any hereditary curse or evil influence. Christ's blood is setting my family free, and He is blessing us with all the goodness of God. Hallelujah! Amen!"

20

My anointing

Most people in Europe have heard of Jesus Christ, but many assume that 'Christ' is His surname - that He's called Jesus Christ like I'm called Colin Dye.

But 'Christ' is Jesus' title, not His surname. He's Christ Jesus - like some people are Doctor Susan, Professor John, Sergeant Bill or Pastor Bruce.

Christ is the Greek word which describes who Jesus is and what He does. It's the same as the Hebrew word *Messiah*, and it means *Anointed*.

This shows, my friend, that you serve 'Jesus the Anointed'. As *Messiah*, as *Christ*, He was anointed with the Spirit for His ministry - without measure!

Throughout His life on earth, Jesus depended on His Father's anointing for everything. He did this so that you'd know how to live the Spirit-filled life.

John prophesied that Jesus would baptise you in the Spirit and fire. And all four Gospels report that Jesus became the Bearer of the Spirit so that He could become the Baptiser in the Spirit.

This was fulfilled at Pentecost, when Jesus Christ anointed His disciples in Jerusalem with the Holy Spirit. From His place in heaven, the risen ascended Lord received the promise of the Father and poured Him onto the church.

Jesus is still the Baptiser in the Spirit. He still plunges disciples into the Spirit - like you plunge a sponge into a bucket of water. He submerges you in the Spirit, and the Spirit fills every part of you.

The Bible uses several terms to describe this experience - 'receiving the Spirit', 'anointing with the Spirit', 'baptism in the Spirit', and so on. But the fullest term is 'being filled with the Spirit'.

The indwelling Spirit

Jesus fills you with the Spirit so that God's very own Holy Spirit can reside in you, can saturate you, can shape, direct and enable you.

You cannot know God without the Spirit. He convicts you of sin and brings you to Jesus. Then, having brought you to Jesus, there comes a moment when the Spirit takes up His residence in your life.

He brings us the presence, power and purity of God, and He leads us in the knowledge and holiness of God. We owe everything that we have to His anointing and to His presence in our lives.

Dear friend, open your heart today to the wonderful fullness of the Spirit. Let Him fill you afresh. Let Him overwhelm you with His presence. And, right now, draw from Him all the resources you need for your situation and circumstances.

God's words for you

I will give you a new heart and put a new spirit within you; I will take the heart of stone out of your flesh and give you a heart of flesh. I will put My Spirit within you and cause you to walk in My statutes, and you will keep My judgements and do them. *Ezekiel 36:26-27*

It shall come to pass afterward that I will pour out My Spirit on all flesh; your sons and your daughters shall prophesy, your old men shall dream dreams, your young men shall see visions. *Joel 2:28*

Behold! My Servant whom I uphold, my Elect One in whom My soul delights! I have put My Spirit upon Him; He will bring forth justice to the Gentiles. *Isaiah 42:1*

I will pour water on him who is thirsty, and floods on the dry ground; I will pour My Spirit on your descendants, and My blessing on your offspring. *Isaiah 44:3*

The Spirit of the Lord is upon Me, because He has anointed Me to preach the gospel to the poor; He has sent Me to heal the broken-hearted, to proclaim liberty to the captives and recovery of sight to the blind, to set at liberty those who are oppressed; to proclaim the acceptable year of the Lord. *Luke 4:18-19*

God anointed Jesus of Nazareth with the Holy Spirit and with power, who went about doing good and healing all who were oppressed by the devil, for God was with Him. *Acts 10:38*

I will pray the Father, and He will give you another Helper, that He may abide with you for ever - the Spirit of truth, whom the world cannot receive, because it neither sees Him nor knows Him; but you know Him, for He dwells with you and will be in you. *John 14:16-17*

I indeed baptise you with water; but One mightier than I is coming, whose sandal strap I am not worthy to loose. He will baptise you with the Holy Spirit and fire. *Luke 3:16*

Whoever drinks of the water that I shall give him will never thirst. But the water that I shall give him will become in him a fountain of water springing up into everlasting life. *John 4:14*

When the Helper comes, whom I shall send to you from the Father, the Spirit of truth who proceeds from the Father, He will testify of Me. *John 15:26*

I tell you the truth. It is to your advantage that I go away; for if I do not go away, the Helper will not come to you; but if I depart, I will send Him to you. *John 16:7*

He whom God has sent speaks the words of God, for God does not give the Spirit by measure. *John 3:34*

You are not in the flesh but in the Spirit, if indeed the Spirit of God dwells in you. Now if anyone does not have the Spirit of Christ, he is not His. *Romans 8:9*

He who keeps His commandments abides in Him, and He in him. And by this we know that He abides in us, by the Spirit whom He has given us. *1 John 3:24*

You shall receive power when the Holy Spirit has come upon you; and you shall be witnesses to Me in Jerusalem, and in all Judea and Samaria, and to the end of the earth. *Acts 1:8*

He who establishes us with you in Christ and has anointed us is God, who also has sealed us and given us the Spirit in our hearts as a guarantee. *2 Corinthians 1:21-22*

Be filled with the Spirit, speaking to one another in psalms and hymns and spiritual songs, singing and making melody in your heart to the Lord, giving thanks always for all things to God the Father in the name of our Lord Jesus Christ. *Ephesians 5:18-20*

They were all filled with the Holy Spirit and began to speak with other tongues, as the Spirit gave them utterance. *Acts 2:4*

Your faith declaration

"I confess and declare that Jesus is the Christ, the Messiah, the Anointed. He is the Bearer of the Spirit, and He has baptised me in the Spirit. I know that I am filled, saturated and anointed by the Spirit of God. He is in me and I am in Him. Hallelujah!

I recognise the voice of the Spirit. I walk in the ways of the Spirit. I resist the enemy by the power of the Spirit. I rely on the Spirit for everything.

The Holy Spirit is my Helper, my Comforter and my Guide. He is my favourite Teacher and my closest Friend. He stands with me and speaks for me. And I stand with Him and listen to His words.

I declare that I am sensitive to the Spirit's promptings in my spirit. I am careful never to grieve Him or to quench His holy fire.

The Spirit releases God's power within me, and enables me to serve the living God. He gives me access to the Father's grace, and brings God's presence to me.

He is the Spirit of fellowship, and through Him I rejoice in the unity of the Body of Christ. I am His and He is mine! Praise His holy name!"

21

My spiritual mind

In the last chapter, I showed you that the gift of the Spirit is your birthright as a believer. Now we'll consider one of the most important functions of the Spirit in your life. He aims, my friend, to make you completely spiritually-minded.

In the Bible, to be 'spiritual' means only one thing. It means 'having the Holy Spirit.' This is why people who don't believe in Jesus can never be considered truly spiritual.

But you started to become a spiritual person when you believed in Jesus. And when the Spirit entered your life as the indwelling presence of God, you began the process of becoming spiritually minded.

When a sponge is plunged in hot soapy water, the sponge is inevitably cleansed. In the same way, when Jesus plunges you in the Spirit, the living water begins to transform you.

Your spirituality is a precious free-gift from the Father. Don't ever despise it. Take pains never to grieve the Spirit through deliberate acts of sin, or to quench His influence in your life. Remember, you owe every gram of spirituality entirely to God.

Before we were saved, we were deeply carnal people. We didn't appreciate spiritual matters and we had little desire for spiritual things. Our minds were set on worldly concerns and material matters.

But now we have the mind of Christ. We're able to receive the things of God deep in our spirits. The Spirit can show us the secret revelations and mysteries of Christ. This is what it means for you to be spiritually-minded.

The renewing of the mind

Dear friend, do you know that it's the Father's deepest desire for you to be completely transformed into His family likeness? He wants you to be just like Jesus! Despite this, many believers are still being moulded into the image of the world.

How can this be? It's because many believers don't understand how the Spirit works to renew, to transform our minds. The key is *consecration*.

Your mind won't be transformed until you present yourself for consecration upon the altar of God, until you offer yourself as living sacrifice to Him.

When you yield to the Spirit like this, He soon begins to mould your mind to match Christ's mind.

This means that you'll begin to think the same thoughts as the Spirit, to share His opinions, to see matters from His point-of-view. His voice will become clearer, and you'll become far more sensitive to His holy promptings.

As a believer, you simply must be shaped and directed by the Spirit. If your mind is influenced by worldly views and values, you'll know despair and disappointment. But if your mind is guided by the Spirit, you'll enjoy abundant life and peace.

The simple truth, my friend, is that you can't know the good-and-perfect will of God in your life without submitting your mind to the work of the Spirit. There's just no other way.

So yield today to the Spirit's work in your life. Let the mind of Christ have full control of your thoughts and actions. Set your mind on those things that the Spirit esteems - on spiritual rather than material concerns. Give all your desires over to Jesus; and the Spirit, your Helper, will be with you!

God's words for you

By the mercies of God, present your bodies a living sacrifice, holy, acceptable to God, which is your reasonable service. *Romans 12:1*

To be carnally minded is death, but to be spiritually minded is life and peace. *Romans 8:6*

We have the mind of Christ. *1 Corinthians 2:16*

The Father of glory give to you the Spirit of wisdom and revelation in the knowledge of Him, the eyes of your understanding being enlightened. *Ephesians 1:17-18*

Those who live according to the flesh set their minds on the things of the flesh, but those who live according to the Spirit, the things of the Spirit. *Romans 8:5*

Do not be conformed to this world, but be transformed by the renewing of your mind, that you may prove what is the good and acceptable and perfect will of God.
Romans 12:2

If you live according to the flesh you will die; but if by the Spirit you put to death the deeds of the body, you will live.
Romans 8:13

If you were raised with Christ, seek those things which are above, where Christ is, sitting at the right hand of God.
Colossians 3:1

It is the Spirit who gives life; the flesh profits nothing. The words that I speak to you are spirit, and they are life. *John 6:63*

We have received, not the spirit of the world, but the Spirit who is from God, that we might know the things that have been freely given to us by God. *1 Corinthians 2:12*

Are you so foolish? Having begun in the Spirit, are you now being made perfect by the flesh? *Galatians 3:3*

I say then: Walk in the Spirit, and you shall not fulfil the lust of the flesh. *Galatians 5:16*

My sheep hear My voice, and I know them, and they follow Me. *John 10:27*

Thus says the High and Lofty One who inhabits eternity, whose name is Holy: 'I dwell in the high and holy place, with him who has a contrite and humble spirit, to revive the spirit of the humble, and to revive the heart of the contrite ones'. *Isaiah 57:15*

Create in me a clean heart, O God, and renew a steadfast spirit within me. *Psalm 51:10*

The sacrifices of God are a broken spirit, a broken and a contrite heart - these, O God, You will not despise. *Psalm 51:17*

The spirit of a man is the lamp of the Lord, searching all the inner depths of his heart. *Proverbs 20:27*

The Lord God has given Me the tongue of the learned, that I should know how to speak a word in season to him who is weary. He awakens Me morning by morning, He awakens My ear to hear as the learned. *Isaiah 50:4*

Your faith declaration

"As a child of God and a co-heir with Christ, I claim my inheritance in the Spirit. My mind is renewed and my life is being transformed. I am a living sacrifice totally dedicated to the spiritual life.

I confess and declare that my ears are attentive to the voice of God, and my mind is responsive to the desires of His heart. My will is submitted to the purposes of God, and my spirit is alive with the presence of His glory. Every day, my understanding is being enlightened by the revelation of His Spirit.

I have the mind of Christ, who teaches me His thoughts. I hold before me a vision of the Lord, and His splendour fills my eyes. I seek only the things of Christ, and desire only what pleases Him.

I have a broken, contrite heart, and a humble, quiet spirit. I tremble at the majesty of God. I am seated with Christ in the heavenlies, and I set my affections on those things which are above.

I reject the carnal mindedness of fleshly thinking, and embrace the life and peace which comes from living the spiritual life. I now live according to the Spirit, and know that Jesus will present me perfect before the Father at the last Day. Hallelujah!"

22

My spiritual gifting

My dear friend, I'm sure you know that the Holy Spirit is your divine Encourager and Enabler.

The Bible calls Him the 'Parakletos'. This Greek word means that the Spirit comes alongside you both to speak to you *and* to speak for you. He comes to encourage you to serve usefully in the church and the world *and* to enable you to help the hurting people around you.

Nobody plunges a sponge in water just to clean the sponge; they do it so they can use the sponge to clean something else. In the same way, Jesus plunges you in the living water of the Spirit so that you can be used in His hand to transform the world.

You do this by living a Spirit-filled life. When you allow the Spirit to saturate and control you fully, His holy qualities start to shine brightly. *His* self-effacing love, joy, peace, power, purity and humility just radiate from your life.

But the Spirit also helps you to serve God in another important way: He gives you spiritual gifts. These supernatural enablings are not tools which are independent of the Spirit; they are aspects of His own nature and character. He gives you of *Himself* to make Christ known to the world.

But, remember, my friend, His enablings are gifts, not rewards. They're proofs of God's grace, not badges of holiness or trophies of maturity.

The Spirit's gifts may develop an existing talent or bring a new ability. It's important to remember, however, that you can do *nothing* for God's kingdom without the help of the Spirit.

The Bible mentions many 'grace-enablings' of the Spirit. Because they are aspects of the Spirit, they're given to *all* Spirit-filled believers. He gives the particular aspect of His nature that you need for the particular task that He's guiding you to fulfil.

As *Parakletos*, the Spirit stands with you and directs you to speak or serve in a particular situation. Then, as *Parakletos*, He stands with you to speak and serve through you in that situation. He doesn't give you a present, and leave you to use it when-and-how you see fit! He gives you *Himself* and expects you always to depend fully on Him.

The Spirit's gifts are meant to build the body of Christ. Like the Spirit, they're given for the benefit of others and not for the promotion of yourself. So please take great care never to misuse an enabling.

His gifts are also meant to witness to Jesus in the world. You simply cannot be an effective witness to Jesus without the Spirit, and His gifts help you to serve more skilfully in mission.

The Spirit's first 'grace-enabling' is usually the ability to pray in a new language. This is a key sign of the Spirit's presence in you. If you've never received this gift, ask Him for it today. Jesus will fill you with His Spirit, and you will pray to the Father in a new spiritual language! Hallelujah!

There are many more signs of the Spirit's presence. He wants you to prophecy, to speak His words with clarity and power. This can be formally, in church, or informally, in your daily life.

He wants you to reveal His healing power, His faith, and His ability to work miracles. And, don't forget, God uses *anyone* who is willing to believe - ordinary believers, raw recruits, seasoned soldiers, small children, senior citizens, even you!

People often overlook the church, but they have to sit up and take notice when a Spiritually-gifted church moves in the power and demonstration of the Spirit. They might persecute you. Or they might be saved. But they certainly won't ignore you!

Never has the need in the nations been so great as now. And God is responding to this need by commissioning an army of willing servants who're ready for a dynamic mission of love and self-sacrifice - and by filling them with His own divine presence and enabling.

My dear friend, it's time for you to rise in the Spirit's power. It's time for you to enlist in His army, to sign up for service, to answer His call to mission. Seek God now for His enabling. It's time for you to reveal Him to the people around you.

God's words to you

When He ascended on high, He led captivity captive, and gave gifts to men. *Ephesians 4:8*

The manifestation of the Spirit is given to each one for the profit of all. *1 Corinthians 12:7*

You shall receive power when the Holy Spirit has come upon you; and you shall be witnesses to Me in Jerusalem, and in all Judea and Samaria, and to the end of the earth.
Acts 1:8

These signs will follow those who believe: In My name they will cast out demons; they will speak with new tongues; they will take up serpents; if they drink anything deadly, it will by no means hurt them; they will lay hands on the sick, and they will recover. *Mark 16:17-18*

Earnestly desire the best gifts. *1 Corinthians 12:31*

Having then gifts differing according to the grace that is given to us, let us use them: if prophecy, let us prophesy in proportion to all our faith; or ministry, let us use it in our ministering; he who teaches in teaching; he who exhorts, in exhortation; he who gives, with liberality; he who leads, with diligence; he who shows mercy, with cheerfulness.
Romans 12:6-8

To one is given the word of wisdom through the Spirit, to another the word of knowledge through the same Spirit; to another faith by the same Spirit, to another gifts of healing by the same Spirit; to another the working of miracles, to another prophecy, to another discerning of spirits, to another different kinds of tongues, to another the interpretation of tongues; but one and the same Spirit works all these things, distributing to each one individually as He wills. *1 Corinthians 12:8-11*

If anyone speaks, let him speak as the oracles of God. If anyone ministers, let him do it as with the ability which God supplies, that in all things God may be glorified through Jesus Christ, to whom belong the glory and the dominion forever and ever. Amen. *1 Peter 4:11*

Your faith declaration

"I confess and declare that the Lord Jesus Christ has called me to be His obedient servant; to serve Him in His royal household, and to serve with Him by washing the feet of the needy.

I have been saved from a life of futility to walk in the good works of fruitfulness, that God prepared for me before the foundation of the world.

I am living a Spirit-filled life, and am allowing the Spirit to control me fully. I can do nothing without His help and guidance. But with His gracious enabling, I can do everything He calls me to do.

When the Spirit directs me to serve, He provides me with His wisdom, His words, His power, His gifts, His abilities. I depend on Him and He works through me. We serve together in partnership.

I am a witness to the Lord. I live and walk in the Spirit, and am revealing Jesus' sacrificial love and healing power, His gracious forgiveness and holy purity, His crucified death and resurrection life.

I only speak what He says, do what He commands, go where He sends. I am His humble and devoted servant. Praise His holy name."

23

My mission

At the beginning of time, when the Father created the world by the Word of His power, He already had you in mind. Long before He filled the universe with His glory, the Father knew you and loved you and chose you for a great purpose.

Before the first star shone, before Adam was made, before Lucifer rebelled, God set you apart for Himself. Throughout eternity, He's had a special purpose for you which is far more wonderful than you can ever imagine!

You've been called to serve the Lord your God, and to bring Him praise and glory throughout your earthly life. What a fantastic prospect!

When God saved you, He brought you into His eternal purpose for your life. You've a destiny to fulfil, dear friend, and not just in heaven! God has a special purpose for your life right here on earth.

God has prepared you for ministry *and* He's prepared a ministry for you. You were saved to serve! You were saved to shine as a witness to Jesus! This is your purpose, your most-important activity, your life-long calling and mission.

As a believer, you're called to work with-and-for Jesus as His witness. The work of a witness is to produce proof. And the work of Jesus' witnesses is to produce convincing proof that He's truly alive. No wonder Jesus told His disciples to wait for God's power before they tried to witness!

You witness by sharing your faith with others. Jesus saved you, and He can save others too! Tell them your story! Speak about Him wherever you go. Explain how He's transformed your life. Be a real disciple. Become a modern-day fisher of men!

Your mission is to make fruitful disciples, not to collect as many 'decisions' as possible. This involves encouraging other believers. You *are* your brother's keeper. You *must* support those around you. You *dare not* live in spiritual isolation.

Every day, pray for some of your brothers and sisters, and build at least one of them with a word of encouragement. Gently lift those who stumble. Weep with those who weep. Rejoice with those who rejoice. Judge nobody, and bite back any critical thoughts. It's a great mission - sharing with Jesus in building and growing His church.

Of course, you can't do this without being in a living relationship with a group of believers. If you're not part of a local church, find one soon. If you're not a member of your church, become one this week. Make sure that you function properly in the bit of the body that He's called you to.

As you come to the end of this book, let me ask you one last question. How's your service? It's hard to lose at tennis if you serve well, and the same is true in the Christian life. You're called to serve God patiently, joyfully, humbly, sacrifically, powerfully, effectively and faithfully.

So be zealous in your ministry with-and-for Him. And remember that God's abundant blessings come to you *so that* you can be an extravagant blessing to others.

Go on, my friend, get on with your mission - for God Himself is with you.

God's words to you

Follow Me, and I will make you fishers of men.
Matthew 4:19

The harvest truly is great, but the labourers are few; therefore pray the Lord of the harvest to send out labourers into His harvest. *Luke 10:2*

Go therefore and make disciples of all the nations, baptising them in the name of the Father and of the Son and of the Holy Spirit, teaching them to observe all things that I have commanded you; and lo, I am with you always, even to the end of the age. *Matthew 28:19-20*

You shall receive power when the Holy Spirit has come upon you; and you shall be witnesses to Me in Jerusalem, and in all Judea and Samaria, and to the end of the earth.
Acts 1:8

Before I formed you in the womb I knew you; before you were born I sanctified you; I ordained you a prophet to the nations. *Jeremiah 1:5*

Have I not commanded you? Be strong and of good courage; do not be afraid, nor be dismayed, for the Lord your God is with you wherever you go. *Joshua 1:9*

I am the vine, you are the branches. He who abides in Me, and I in him, bears much fruit; for without Me you can do nothing. *John 15:5*

I myself am confident concerning you, my brethren, that you also are full of goodness, filled with all knowledge, able also to admonish one another. *Romans 15:14*

By this My Father is glorified, that you bear much fruit; so you will be My disciples. *John 15:8*

I thank Christ Jesus our Lord who has enabled me, because He counted me faithful, putting me into the ministry. *1 Timothy 1:12*

From whom the whole body, joined and knit together by what every joint supplies, according to the effective working by which every part does its share, causes growth of the body for the edifying of itself in love. *Ephesians 4:16*

Take heed to the ministry which you have received in the Lord, that you may fulfil it. *Colossians 4:17*

Brethren, if a man is overtaken in any trespass, you who are spiritual restore such a one in a spirit of gentleness, considering yourself lest you also be tempted. *Galatians 6:1*

Bear one another's burdens, and so fulfil the law of Christ. *Galatians 6:2*

Even the Son of Man did not come to be served, but to serve, and to give His life a ransom for many. *Mark 10:45*

When you have done all those things which you are commanded, say, 'We are unprofitable servants. We have done what was our duty to do.' *Luke 17:10*

Let us consider one another in order to stir up love and good works. *Hebrews 10:24*

Well done, good and faithful servant; you have been faithful over a few things, I will make you ruler over many things. Enter into the joy of your lord. *Matthew 25:23*

Your faith declaration

"I am anointed with God's own Holy Spirit, and I have been set apart for the Master's personal use. I am a vessel of His honour, and His holy treasure abides in an earthen vessel. The excellency of the power belongs entirely to God. To Him be all the praise and honour, by Christ Jesus my Lord.

I confess and declare that I am called by Almighty God to be a witness to Jesus, to be a fisher of men, to be a disciple maker, to be a church builder.

I will fully obey this calling, depending at all times on the anointing and enabling of the Spirit.

I am my brother and sister's keeper. I am wholly committed to the body of Christ. I am a constant encourager. I have renounced all criticism and negative speaking.

I am not ashamed of the gospel of Christ, for it is the power of salvation. I long for all hurting people to experience Christ's saving love, and I take every opportunity to speak about Him.

I hereby dedicate myself completely to the ministry of Jesus, and will serve Him zealously for the rest of my earthly days. To Him be all praise and glory forever. Amen."

Part Three

MORE DECLARATIONS

This final section contains five more declarations for you to declare aloud to yourself, to God and to the principalities and powers.

Don't read them all at one sitting. Take them a day at a time; and return to them often as God leads you by His Spirit.

Remember, God's Word in your mouth is just as powerful as His Word in His mouth. When you speak His words, it's as good as done!

24

The Word

"Your Word, O Lord, is in my mouth, my spirit and my heart. I walk in obedience to Your Word, observing all that is written in it. Therefore my way will prosper and I will have good success.

I hide Your Word in my heart so that I might not sin against You. By the Word of Your lips, I keep myself from the path of the destroyer.

I am strong through the Word abiding in me. By it, I overcome the wicked one. I grasp the sword of the Spirit, and use it to destroy every evil plan and device of the enemy.

I confess Your Word and hold to its truth at all times. I put my trust in Your Word. I believe its

26

rgiving others

ner in heaven, I acknowledge that I urt by ....(name the person pecific circumstances involved).

o come to me, and to heal me of this Please bring me the comfort and the of the Holy Spirit, in Jesus' name.

her, as You have forgiven me, I now .... for his/her part in this pain.

him/her from any resentment, any udes, any hurtful thoughts, any critical s which I have made against him/her.

every truth. I hold to its every promise. I obey its every instruction. I depend on its every provision.

Every part of Your Word is true and abides for ever. Your Word is exalted above all things and is forever settled in heaven.

Your Word produces Your life in me. Through Your exceeding great and precious promises, I have been made a partaker of Your divine nature. I live by the faith that comes from hearing Your Word, and by that faith I live on every Word which proceeds from Your mouth.

Your Word is a lamp to my feet and a light to my path. My way is cleansed by the Word from every impurity. Your Word sanctifies me and sets me apart. Your holy will brings me great reward.

I give my full attention to Your words, keeping them in the midst of my heart - for they are life to those who find them and health to all their flesh.

I declare that Your Word has free course to accomplish in me, and to perform through me, whatever is pleasing in Your sight. To You be all honour and glory. Amen."

25

The Blood

"Holy Father, I thank you for the precious blood of Jesus - for it is as pure as the blood of a lamb which is without any blemish or spot.

I thank You that the blood pleads for me, asking for Your mercy and grace. I thank You that the blood gives me access into Your holy presence, and that it has purchased my complete salvation.

I now declare and confess all the Word says that His blood has done for me.

I am justified and forgiven by the shed blood of Jesus. I am sanctified, wholly set apart to God, by the once-and-for-all offering of Christ.

I revoke any curse-like pronouncements that I have made, either verbally, or in writing, or in my thoughts, against ....

Gracious, generous Father, I now ask You to bless and prosper .... in everything he/she does.

Forgive me for the bitterness that I have sinfully held against him/her. Cleanse me from this defilement. Heal me from all its physical, emotional and spiritual effects.

In Jesus' mighty name, please deliver me from any satanic bondages which have come as a result of my bitterness.

I ask this prayer, with absolute confidence, in Jesus' forgiving name. Amen."

27

Deliverance from evil

"Victorious Lord and Father, You have ordained praise to silence the foe and the avenger. Therefore, I offer You high praises and execute Your written Word of judgement against Your enemy.

If You had not been on my side when the enemy rose against me, then I would have been swallowed alive. If You had not been on my side when his wrath was kindled against me, then the waters would have gone over my soul. Blessed be the Lord, who has not given me as prey to the teeth of the enemy. The snare is broken and I have escaped.

I know that the devil can gain no advantage over me because I resist him by standing firm in the faith of my God. I submit to God in humility, I resist the devil, and he flees from me - in Jesus' name.

I am not ignorant of Satan's many schemes to deceive, to tempt, to accuse, to steal, to spoil and to hurt me. But I also know that Jesus was manifested to destroy all the works of the evil one.

I put on, and I continue to live in, the full armour of God. I rest under the safety, the protection and the security of the powerful name of Jesus Christ.

I walk in the light as Christ is in the light. And He cleanses me from every sin. Praise His holy name.

I confess and declare that the living Lord Jesus has given me His power over the enemy. And so I take authority over - I tread down completely - every spiritual serpent, every spiritual scorpion, every evil spirit, every wicked device of the devil.

Nothing shall by any means harm me, no weapon formed against me shall ever prevail, for God my Father delivers me from the evil one as I confess His magnificent name.

My help is in the name of the Lord, who made heaven and earth. His victorious presence is with me at all times. Hallelujah! Amen!"

28

God's watchman

"Father God, I come before You and take my place on the high walls over ....(name your city, town or village). As Your watchman, I stand at my post and acknowledge that I am called, anointed and positioned by You. Unless You watch over the city, the watchmen guard it in vain.

I confess that I am crucified with Christ, and I submit completely to my Father's will. I am born of the Spirit, led by the Spirit, and filled with His presence and power.

I walk in step with the Spirit and surrender to His full control. I die to my own thoughts, emotions, feelings, desires and ambitions.

I declare that I am awake, alert and fully attentive to the voice of God. My eyes and ears are open and anointed to see and hear. I am self-controlled, vigilant, and faithful in intercession. I watch and pray in the Spirit with all kinds of prayers, petitions and supplications - which I offer with thanksgiving. For my God is able to do far above what I ask or imagine, according to His power at work in me.

I lift my voice to God. For Your people's sake, I will not be silent. I will cry to You night and day until You make Your people a praise in the earth.

I am a servant of Christ, and I proclaim that the will of the Lord will prosper. The Word of the Lord will prevail. It will accomplish the purpose for which it is sent.

I bless the Body of Christ, in all its places and many expressions. I uphold the unity of the Spirit in the bond of peace. I watch in hope for the Lord's coming. I wait for God my Saviour.

My Father watches over me, He neither slumbers nor sleeps. He preserves me, keeps me safe, and will present me faultless at the day of Jesus Christ.

I now declare that I will willingly serve Him, wherever He bids me go, whatever He commands me to do, all the rest of my days. Amen."

Other books in this

LIVING WORD SERIES include:

- Prayer that gets answers
- Household salvation
- The unlimited power of the blood

For a full catalogue of Colin Dye ministry products, please contact:

Dovewell Mail Order
PO Box 9161
London
W3 6GS
England

Tel: 0171 727 8684
Fax: 0171 727 8716
e mail: ken-temp@dircon.co.uk
web site: http/www.ken-temp.org.uk